STOPPING PLACES
ALONG DUXBURY ROADS

Stopping Places
Along Duxbury Roads

MARGERY L. MACMILLAN

THE DUXBURY RURAL AND HISTORICAL SOCIETY
Duxbury, Massachusetts

To paraphrase author and historian David McCullough: To some history is a thing of the past, but unless we record what occurs today there will be no history for tomorrow.

This book is only the first 350 years of Duxbury's social life portrayed through the town's historic houses. Perhaps a sequel should be forthcoming in another one hundred years.

Cover: Lithograph of the Standish Shore Company by Armstrong and Company, courtesy William S. Waters. Design by Cornelia Boynton.

Printed in the United States of America

International Standard Book Number 0-941859-01-0

Library of Congress Catalog Card Number 90-080865

To Ladd

Be his
My special thanks, whose even-balanced soul
From first youth tested up to extreme old age,
Business could not make dull, nor Passion wild;
Who saw life steadily and saw it whole.

Matthew Arnold

Preface

On retiring in 1984 after 35 years of dedicated service to the town, Duxbury's able Town Historian, Dorothy Wentworth, suggested that volunteers from the Rural and Historical Society pursue selected research topics that she had not had time to investigate as thoroughly as she would have liked. Among her suggestions was the story of houses, now privately owned, that had once served as hostelries of one kind or another. As my own house was once a tearoom, this subject piqued my curiosity and I became the first volunteer.

The task was like a treasure hunt. Mrs. Wentworth presented me with a few clues, but most of the pieces to the puzzle were hidden. My suppressed desire to become a sleuth surfaced and over the next five years I worked on ferreting out answers to most of the mysteries.

The solutions to the puzzle were provided by the many wonderful Duxbury residents who graciously welcomed me and cheerfully answered my many questions. Often my visits were followed up by telephone calls when I would think of a new inquiry, or better still, when my new friends suddenly remembered old facts. It is they, whose names appear in the acknowledgments, who have made this book possible, for the social history of a town is best revealed by those who live here. With patience, a researcher can find necessary facts in town records and the like, but attitudes, points of view and that much needed ingredient, humor, are only uncovered by direct communication with individual inhabitants.

M.L.M.

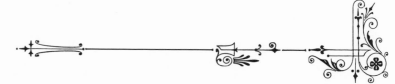

Acknowledgments

There are so many people who made this book possible that your names appear elsewhere. I am grateful to all of you.

Sincere thanks also go to those who answered my questioning letters sent to many parts of the United States and who voluntarily supplied more information than I sought.

A few people must have particular recognition: Dorothy Wentworth for constant long-distance assistance; Anthony Kelso, who so generously permitted me to use his definitive research on the Myles Standish Hotel; Robert Dente for his loan of many postcards; Mrs. Nina Burns for her assistance on the Milepost; Miss Georgiana Winsor concerning the Winsor House; Constance Fraser and Diana Seamans for their letters relating to Hall's Tavern; Mildred Glass and Russell Edwards for their incredible recall; Mrs. Nancy Oates and many others at the Duxbury Town Hall for their cheerful research assistance; Sabina Crosby for copying everything ad infinitum, and Anthony Baker and Frances Nichols for their photographic work. Finally, my endless gratitude goes to Katherine Pillsbury, Robert Hale, and Anthony Kelso for their thoughtful vetting of this manuscript.

M.L.M.

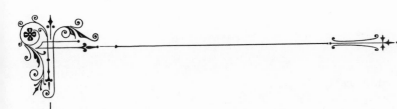

Table of Contents

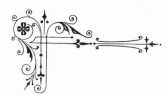

HOTELS AND INNS

BOARDING HOUSES

TEAROOMS

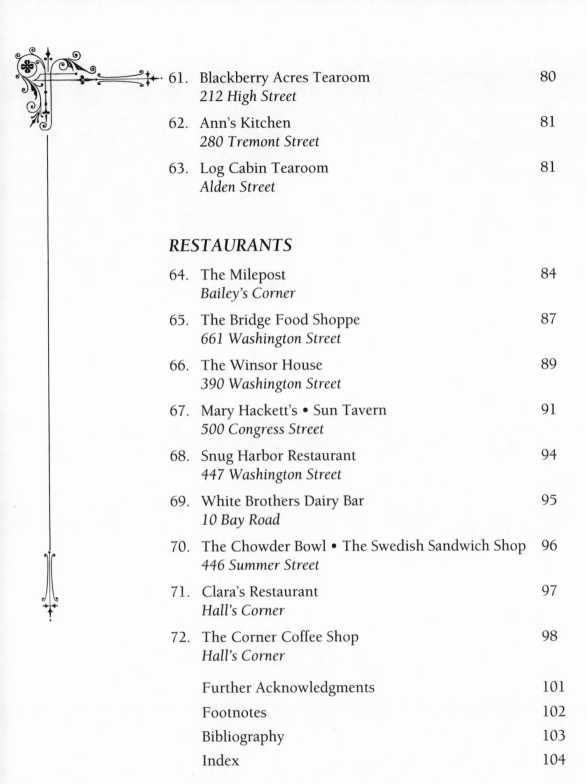

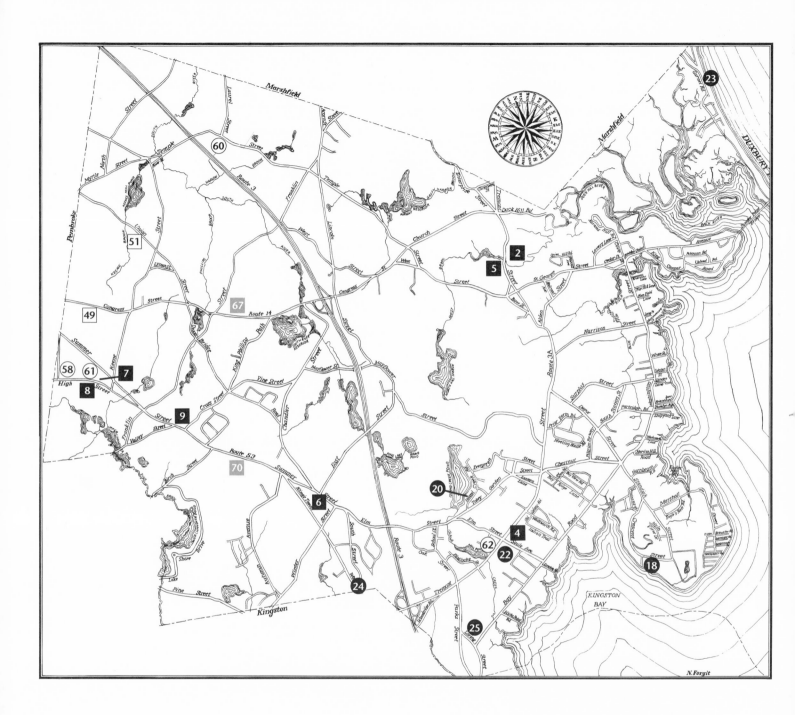

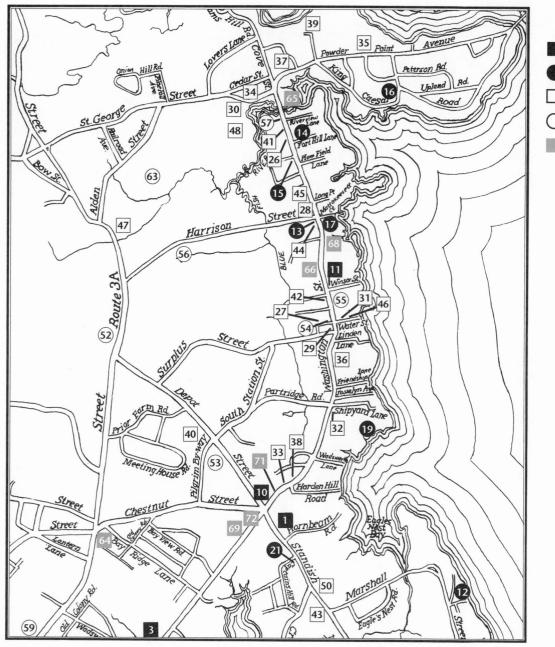

KEY

◼ Taverns

● Hotels / Inns

◻ Boarding Houses

○ Tearooms

▪ Restaurants

Introduction

In the seventeenth century when roads were rudimentary and traveling on foot or horseback especially arduous, weary travelers would seek the warmth of spirits and nourishment of victuals at ordinaries and taverns to whisk away their fatigue. Ordinances were passed requiring that hostelries be established for the comfort of the people, but at the same time the authorities tried to keep close control over both those who ran the taverns and their patrons.

Webster defines a tavern as "a place where anyone may drop in for a drink or a meal." An ordinary, on the other hand, is "a place where regular meals are served and often used for gambling after the guests have dined." Dr. Sylvester Kelley, who once lived in Duxbury's "Old Ordinary" prefers the name "ordinary" over "tavern," because, as he says, " it implies more dignity."

Taverns or ordinaries provided accommodations for travelers and served as local gathering places as well. There the patrons could buy food and drink to be consumed on the premises. In fact, the authorities encouraged the serving of food along with drink because the food made it less likely that the patrons would drink too much.

Nevertheless, the authorities also licensed local retail establishments which were more like package stores where "strong waters" were sold.

When the first taverns and retail establishments were licensed in the seventeenth century, Duxbury was principally a farming community, so the population remained relatively stable. However, following the Revolutionary War, as the town grew into a major ship building center, there was a large influx of laborers and other workers. Accommodations were needed not only for travelers but also for the shipwrights, sailmakers, and others who came to town to help build and outfit vessels. Some of the houses they occupied were already here; others were newly built. Imposing houses were also being built for the new elite in town, the master mariners, sea captains, and merchants who chose to live along Washington Street close by the shipyards along the bay. If a carpenter could assist in building a ship, he could also build a house, and a mighty fine one, too.

To serve the hard-drinking workers, taverns proliferated. One corner of town, by Surplus and Washington streets, became known as Sodom, because of the number of drinking establishments in the vicinity.

By mid-nineteenth century, after the shipbuilding enterprises had moved to deeper water ports, Duxbury's economy turned downward. Fortunately, with the advent of railroads, our little seaside town did not lay dormant for very long. Duxbury rebounded as a popular summer resort for city people who came to be refreshed by the sea. Visitors enjoyed the clean sea air and the abundance of fresh garden produce which was always on the menus of the hotels and inns which flourished at the time. The Standish Hotel also offered healthy spring water from the historic Standish Spring.

In spite of the vacationers interest in health, the town fathers were still concerned with regulating the consumption of liquor. In the 1884 *Town Report* they wrote, "It will be seen . . . your selection, by vote of the town . . . How far it is believed the licensing the sale of intoxicating liquors has added to the prosperity of the town, the quiet of families and the good of the rising generation, we hope will be expressed by no uncertain vote at the annual meeting in April next."

From 1891 to 1913 the town voted to remain dry except for one notable exception in 1894 when the vote was 79 for and 70 against the sale of liquor. That must have been a memorable year! For several years after 1913, no vote was taken, but with the advent of national prohibition in 1919, none was needed. Just how many local establishments served liquor illegally during Prohibition cannot be accurately measured, for much of the information comes by hearsay and rumor. Suffice it to say that contraband liquor did arrive on these shores and some was consumed locally without too much interference from the authorities.

Both before and after Prohibition, many Duxbury ladies, often widows, were concerned with making ends meet. They were usually homebodies and excellent cooks. Those whose houses were large enough for overnight guests opened them for summer boarders. Others, with smaller houses often started tearooms with gift shops filled with home crafts to add to their income. Local summer residents, guests at inns, and day trippers from surrounding communities enjoyed spending leisurely afternoons at Duxbury's pleasant tearooms. During Prohibition these tearooms flourished as they provided healthy, nonalcholic refreshment, especially for ladies.

Finally, when even the hotels were gone and most of the inns had become private homes, a need developed for full time restaurants in Duxbury. Some of these, first started in the 1920s, are still operating, while others have come and gone.

Since 1964 when Route 3 was completed, Duxbury has become almost completely residential. Many of the inns, taverns, boarding houses and tearooms which once served travelers, working men, and vacationers are now private residences. This book will serve to shed some light on the interesting stories and history connected with these buildings.

Taverns

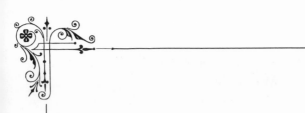he first tavern in Duxbury was located close to the center of town, near the Chestnut Street meeting house. Men gathering there for town meeting or military drill could enjoy the conviviality at the ordinary.

Duxbury's early taverns were carefully regulated. Only one man at a time was licensed to run an ordinary, and that man was supposed to be of high moral character.

From the start the New Plymouth Colony enacted strict laws concerning the sale of "strong waters."[1] In 1636 the law read, "that none be suffered to retale wine, strong water or beere either within doors or without except in Inns or victualling houses . . ." However, in 1662 allowances were made "for such entente and Purposes as to releave the weak and sicke . . ."[2] Records show this law and others designed to control the consumption of alcohol were occasionally broken. Most Duxbury citizens farmed on large tracts of land, so a person would have had to go some distance to get to an ordinary or retailer to purchase spirits. Also, it was easy for a farmer to grow barley to make malt for home brew or to let his cider ferment.

By the eighteenth century Duxbury taverns were being built to accommodate travelers along the routes between Plymouth and Boston, especially on what is now High Street. After stagecoaches became the preferred means of inland travel, inns were needed along the way as resting places for both travelers and their horses.

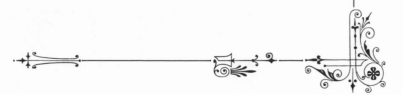

Francis Sprague's Ordinary

1 Formerly in the Vicinity of Standish Street and Hornbeam Road
1638

Constant Southworth's

2 Millbrook
17th Century

Certain individuals who were supposedly "discreet and sober minded" were licensed to sell wine and beer to their neighbors. Francis Sprague was the first resident of Duxbury to be granted a license on October 1, 1638 "to keepe a victualling on Duxburrow Side."[3] If travelers appeared at the Sprague farmhouse they were probably offered lodging for the night. Women were given any available beds while the men slept by the fire.

Unfortunately, Sprague was anything but sober and discreet. He was fined several times for "drinking overmuch, beating William Bassett's servant, killing a mare and selling contraband weapons to the Indians."[4]

By 1669 Francis Sprague's son John held the license. A chip off the old block, he spent time in the stocks for "drinking, gameing and uncivil revelling."[5]

Francis Sprague's house could be called an ordinary because of the victuals served there. Constant Southworth, who lived in the Millbrook area, William Collier, who is thought to have lived near Morton's Hole, and Samuel Seabury, whose house was in the Island Creek area, were retailers who sold liquor over the counter.

For many years Constant Southworth was Plymouth Colony Treasurer. He also served as Commissary General at the beginning of King Philip's War. Southworth bought Duxbury's first gristmill at Millbrook from William Hillier in 1646. In 1648 he was allowed to sell wine from his house nearby.

*Francis Sprague's ordinary was in the Harden Hill area, not far from the meeting house.
(Robert Dente)*

William Collier's
Formerly near Morton's Hole
17th Century

Samuel Seabury's
Island Creek
17th Century

William Collier had been a brewer in London. A gentleman, he was one of the wealthy merchants who financed Plymouth Colony. He served the colony as assistant governor and as a commissioner of the United Colonies of New England, a loose federation formed between Plymouth Colony, Massachusetts Bay, and New Haven to counter Indian threats in 1643.

Collier was granted tracts of land in Duxbury both at North Hill and near Morton's Hole, where he probably lived. In 1660 he was granted a license to sell "strong waters."[6] In contrast to his neighbor Francis Sprague, Collier was a God-fearing, law-abiding member of the colony.

Duxbury's third retailer, Samuel Seabury, Sr, lived in a house with a "roof nearly touching the ground."[7] (This steep framing, known as a saltbox locally, is medieval in origin and afforded one-half story more room.) Seabury was licensed in 1678 "to sell liquors unto such sober minded naighboors, as he shall think meet, soe as he sell a quantie of a gallon att a time and not in smaller quantities by retaile to the occupationing of drukenes."[8] As no mention is made of how frequently a neighbor could purchase the "quantie of a gallon att a time," those with authority to grant liquor licenses may have made curbing the "wickedness of Drukenes" more difficult for themselves.

Mr. Seabury and Mr. Francis West were part of the local constabulary at the time. They were appointed by the court in 1665 "to have inspection of the ordinaries and other suspected places"[9] in Duxbury. The phrase "other suspected places" raises the suspicion that the inhabitants of Duxbury did not always adhere to the law concerning spirits!

Samuel Seabury, inspector of ordinaries in the 17th century, lived near Island Creek Pond.

The Old Ordinary

5

1296 Tremont Street
17th Century

The house always known as the Old Ordinary is in Millbrook. Previously the house of Dr. Sylvester Kelley, it is now the residence of Mr. and Mrs. Joseph Shea. The house is probably seventeenth century, but has not yet been dateboarded.

Early in the nineteenth century employees of the woolen mill boarded in this house. Probably, workers from the fulling mill which preceded it lived there a half century earlier as well. In 1914 the house was purchased by Anice Bolton. She ran it as a boarding house which she called The Wayside Inn. When Duxbury's water main was put in, the men digging the trenches were housed here.

By 1918 the property was acquired by James T. and Nathaniel Ford. As the large Ford store was nearby, the ordinary was a fine place to house some of the employees. The Fords often leased the house, and at one time it was rented by an odd Frenchman who kept horses, cows, and pigs in the cellar with hens and chickens clucking on the first floor. He was a bit of a wild man with a fearsome temper. He was known to have thrown axes, which fortunately missed his wife, but left many marks that can still be seen on the walls of the house.

During renovations Mr. and Mrs. Shea found innumerable scraps of leather within the walls which indicates that the house was also the site of a cottage industry: shoemaking.

When the nearby Ford store burned in 1921, fortunately this wonderful Duxbury landmark was saved.

One of the few early ordinaries still standing in Duxbury faces south off Tremont Street in the Millbrook area. (Above: Fran Nichols)

Cobb's Tavern • The Briars

6
110 Summer Street
18th Century

Robert Sampson started a tavern in his home after his marriage in 1734, and by 1749 he was listed as an inn-keeper in a deed. When Sampson died in 1775, the property passed on to his son, Noah Sampson. Asa Chandler probably ran the tavern during Noah's ownership. By 1833 it was known as Cobb's Tavern, as it was run by Lemuel Cobb, Jr. For a period of time at the end of the nineteenth century the house was a private home.

In about 1915, Mrs. Lantz Whitehead purchased the property and renamed it *The Briars*. She brought "city ideas" from Boston, and gambling became part of her establishment.

One day while workmen were renovating the house, Mrs. Whitehead had an accident. A floorboard gave way and she fell through part way. Her clothes became caught over her head, and while she dangled, the workmen dawdled. Finally, in exasperation she cried, "To heck with modesty, get me out of here!"

In the 1920s The Briars was operated by Louis Nardi, who was famous for his home-brewed Italian wine. The Elks met there regularly and according to Wendell Phillips, who lived nearby, a large kitchen with a hotel range was added so that food could also be served.

Gradually The Briars became more of a speakeasy than a restaurant. Since this was during Prohibition, the word of a raid would send all hands flying to the garden carrying bottles to be quickly buried. One raid led to Mr. Nardi's downfall. He had one good eye; the other, according to Mr. Phillips, "rolled around and sometimes faced the world and sometimes not." Mr. Nardi pulled a gun on a policeman who couldn't tell where he was aiming. This imprudent act proved too much for the Law, and The Briars ceased to operate.

On July 2, 1986 this historic tavern was gutted by fire while undergoing restoration. Fortunately, John Ferreira, the present owner, has rebuilt the house.

This eighteenth-century tavern originally called Cobb's is on Summer Street in the Chandlerville area. (Right: Philip O. Swanson)

(Top: Nancy Glass, bottom: Fran Nichols)

Pegged together of oak and pine,
  Wide floor boards polished to shine.
Built by neighbors and friends who met
  In friendship, or to pay a debt.
Central chimney, a masterpiece,
  With firepaces and flues complete.
Hand-hewn beams to chimney braced,
  And with grooved wood deftly cased.
Small window panes of wavy hue,
  That dazzle when the sun shines through.
Oil Lamps cast a yellow gleam,
  Hanging from the center beam.
Every bit a rugged home,
  One I'm proud to call my own.

— NANCY LOUISE GLASS

Loring Tavern

7   180 High Street
William Loring
1767

Seventeenth-century taverns were located in the tavernkeepers' own homes, but by the eighteenth century larger taverns were being built to serve travelers along the main roads between towns. The King's Highway, or Bay Path, the principal inland road between Plymouth and Boston, followed a route through Duxbury along what is now High Street.

In 1767 William Loring married Alethea Alden, a great-granddaughter of John and Priscilla Alden. With superior workmanship he built for her a two-story house set well back from the road. Mr. Loring must have had several considerations in mind when he built such a large house for his bride, for it soon had a swinging sign in front advertising, "Loring Tavern."

The tavern undoubtedly served as a stagecoach stop, for there was ample room on the 40-acre property for both man and beast. Many guests arrived on horseback. Over the stalls in the old barn out back are painted the names of horses—Fan, John, and Fred. Perhaps these animals served as relays for the stagecoach teams that changed horses at the tavern.

The present owners, Mrs. Nancy MacFarlane Glass and her brother, John MacFarlane, have read letters about the house dating back to the tavern days. In 1844 the West Duxbury Post Office was located in the east parlor, and in 1929 the house once again served as post office when Mrs. Glass was postmistress.

Voices of past travelers and former owners still seem to echo throughout this fine old house. Nancy Glass assured us it will continue to stand for at least another two hundred years when she was heard to remark, "This is such a magical world, why shouldn't the future be bright!"

Lowden Tavern
8 203 High Street
Mid-1700s

Delano Tavern and Store
9 Summer Street

Like Loring Tavern, Lowden Tavern was situated on the Bay Path, or King's Highway, now High Street. On February 11, 1772 Lowden Tavern "took fire and there being a large quantity of flax in an upper chamber and the weather dry and windy, the house was consumed with nearly all the contents."[10] Richard Lowden rebuilt the tavern almost immediately on the original site. The antiquity of the building is best revealed by the cellar stairs which are constructed of tree trunks and notched, flattened logs in which treads are fitted. The foundation is of fieldstone.[11]

Richard Lowden, tavernkeeper, died in 1777, leaving the substantial estate of 781 pounds.

After Lowden Tavern burned in 1772, an almost identical house was built the following year. (Eleanor B. Sprowl) Right: Lowden's Tavern today (Fran Nichols)

On the road to Boston near Four Mile Hill (on Route 53, just beyond Osborn's Store), John and Ruth Delano kept a store and tavern after their marriage in 1774. John Delano died in 1825 but his wife, like so many widows, continued her husband's business after his death. The store probably sold such staples as sugar, molasses, and rum. Some of this rum was listed in an auction of John Delano's goods.

Ruth Delano owned land on both sides of the Boston Road. She continued running the business until 1845 when she decided to sell the property across the road from the store to Ichabod Delano, provided the store was moved to the new site.

The original site of the Delano store and tavern, across Summer Street, was later the property of the Whiting Milk Company.

The tavern itself was razed in 1966–1967.

Hall's Tavern

10 Formerly on the Corner of
Washington and Depot Streets

c. 1810

One hundred forty years after the Spragues kept their taverns, the Hall's Corner area was once again the site of an inn. Captain Daniel Hall had his house built there circa 1810, on the foundation of a previous house. One of the most beautifully constructed and well-proportioned buildings in Duxbury at the time, Daniel Hall's house stood on the corner of Washington and Depot streets. A family letter offers some more of the history of the house.

> Joshua Hall, Daniel Hall's father, owned a large lot of land more or less all in one lot from the shore to the old burying ground. Daniel Hall lived in the old house 12 years after he was married which was in 1798 a year after his father died. D. Hall built over the old cellar . . . using lumber he purchased down east and seasoning it at the shore for a whole year . . . and built this house and cellar the whole bigness of the house.

The builder is unknown, but his superior craftsmanship was apparent inside and out. The house was painted white with contrasting green quoinwork. A visitor would enter through the handsome doorway topped by a fan-shaped window. He would admire the cornices and wainscotting, embellished with inlaid mahogany in the parlor and living room. A unique feature of the house was a bull's-eye glass inserted in one of the top corner panels of the door that separated the kitchen-dining area from the parlor. This feature probably enabled innkeeper Hall to ascertain whether guests still remained in the parlor, without interrupting them.

Captain Daniel retired early from the sea and played the role of innkeeper until his death in 1847. During this time a young gentleman, enroute to his wedding in Plymouth, spent a night at Hall's Tavern. He remarked, while looking out the window, that he might have seen his lady's house, except for Captain's Hill on the Standish Shore. The young man reflected that the hill would be a wonderful place to build a monument some day. When the cornerstone of the

Hall's Tavern was at Hall's Corner where the Exxon Station is now located. (Anthony Kelso)

8

Miss Caroline Hall, the last of the Halls to live in the Captain Daniel Hall House. (Virginia Stasinos). At right, Hall's Tavern as it appears in Cambridge.

Myles Standish Monument was laid in 1872, the young gentleman's prophesy proved to be true.

The last of the Halls to live in the house was Captain Daniel's daughter, Caroline, who died in 1892. Mrs. Virginia Stasinos, a Hall descendent, reports that her family thought that Caroline was a forbidding lady. A descendent of Myles Standish, Miss Hall helped convince the skeptics concerning the exact location of Myles Standish's grave in the Old Burying Ground.

Mr. Henry Briggs Chandler, Levi Cushing's maternal grandfather, purchased the Hall house in 1903. Levi's mother, Helen B. Cushing, and her sister, Minerva Sherman, inherited it from their father in 1923.

For sixteen years starting in 1906, Mr. and Mrs. Charles F. Shirley ("Doc Shirley") rented the old tavern. Their oldest son was born there, and Mr. Shirley's sister, Helen, was married in the south parlor to Howe S. Newell, a teacher at the Powder Point School.

After this period, the house was unoccupied for some time and fell into disrepair. In 1930, Mrs. Cecil E. Fraser, an authority on early American decoration and antiques and a colonial-house enthusiast, persuaded her husband, a Harvard Business School professor, to purchase Hall's Tavern for $4500.

The tavern was flaked, which meant it was carefully dismantled and numbered piece by piece to be reassembled in a new location. During the flaking process, early foreign coins were found plastered in the walls. Among these was a lead token, dated 1805, with Nelson's head on one side and a full-rigged ship on the other. It took 35 truck loads, insured by Lloyds of London, to move the old tavern to 20 Gray Gardens West in Cambridge, at a cost of $18,850. There the house was reconstructed under the watchful eye of Clarence W. Brazer, a student of colonial architecture and an authority on early American furniture who later married Mrs. Fraser. The house that was once Hall's Tavern in Duxbury still stands in Cambridge and remains a private home.

9

The Cracker Tavern

11 Formerly at the Corner of Winsor
and Washington Streets
John Winsor
1824

The Cracker Tavern once stood on the northeast corner of Winsor and Washington streets in Duxbury village. Unfortunately this beautiful Federal-period house, which had upper and lower galleries on both the east and west ends, was torn down in 1962.

Henry Thoreau wrote in his book *Cape Cod* that "Winsor the tavernkeeper" took him to Clark's Island.[12] Undoubtedly it is John Winsor of the Cracker Tavern to whom he refers.

Daniel Webster, who had a home in Marshfield and who frequented Ford's Store on Tremont Street, is purported to have stayed at the Cracker Tavern. Somewhere in Duxbury there is a photograph of him standing on the upper gallery lifting a tankard, but it has not surfaced recently.

It is not impossible to imagine Webster and Thoreau sharing grog together at the Cracker Tavern. Thoreau appreciated a good tavern for he once wrote: "the Gods who are most interested in the human race preside over the tavern . . . The Tavern will compare favorably with the church. The church is the place where prayers and sermons are delivered, but the tavern is where they are to take effect, and if the former are good, the latter cannot be bad."[13]

Pauline Winsor Wilkinson explained the origin of the tavern's name. "Boys who worked in Boston and who came down for a two-week vacation dubbed it "The Cracker" because at every meal they served large, soft crackers used in clam or fish chowder."[14] It must have been a charming place to stay, for the upper galleries commanded incredible views, especially on the east end facing the water.

Exterior and interior of the fomer Cracker Tavern, torn down in 1962. (Priscilla Hall)

Hotels and Inns

In the mid-nineteenth century the halcyon days of shipbuilding came to an end in Duxbury. New clipper ships and steamboats that required deeper harbors than Duxbury's proved to be too much competition for the town's aging merchant fleet. The local workforce scattered, some to Boston shipyards, others to factories.

At the same time railroads were growing rapidly. Offering more efficient transportation for both people and goods, the railroads sealed the fate of the declining shipbuilding industry. Duxbury became subdued and dispirited, but it would not remain depressed for long.

Duxbury's salvation was its sea and its sand, its high pines and historic houses. Above all, the town's rich history, beginning with her Pilgrim settlers, made it an interesting place to visit then, as it does now.

In 1871 the Duxbury and Cohasset Railroad linked Duxbury with the extensive Old Colony Line which served Boston, Kingston, and Plymouth. Now that the town was accessible, summer people began to arrive, ushering in a new era. The local economy thrived: hotels, inns, and cottages were built. Larger houses were turned into inns, while smaller ones became boarding houses. The railroad provided jobs, and local businesses grew to accommodate the influx of people.

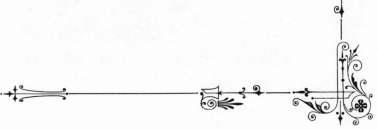

Resort hotels and inns offered retreats for many from steaming cities. Long piazzas filled with rattan rocking chairs lured guests to unwind and relax. Facing the view of the ever-changing ocean and breathing deeply of salt air, the vacationers' spirits rose, their cares vanished, and their tired souls were rejuvenated. With so much to offer, it is not surprising the town soon became a thriving summer resort.

One local enterprise that flourished was the livery business. Henry Briggs owned a stable by the Bluefish River. There he kept the vehicles and horses with which he transported hotel and boarding-house guests to and from the Millbrook and South Duxbury depots. One of the horse-drawn vehicles was a barge called *Martha Washington*. The two smaller carriages were called *Pet* and *What Cheer*. According to Frederick Potter, the latter was so named because it was gaily painted with a circus-wagon motif.

Not all of the summer guests arrived by train. Around the turn of the century horseless carriages began to appear. Virginia Ludwig vividly recalled her mother and father, along with two other children, loading up the Simplex in Medford. Three blow-outs later they arrived at Powder Point Hall in Duxbury.

Summer people had their favorite areas in the town to which they returned year after year. Some had a predilection for Powder Point, others opted for the Standish Shore which was less developed. Still others were happiest on Abrams Hill. There the residents of houses built on higher elevations enjoyed the cooling breezes and view overlooking the marshes.

This is all true today. Generation has followed generation in their love of Duxbury. However, almost all the houses have become year-round residences. Grandparents' houses used only in the summer have now become the permanent homes of their grandchildren.

Although Duxbury's wide open spaces have gone, and new houses dot the horizon, our coastal town is still a treasure. Like a pearl once hidden in an oyster, its secret charm has been discovered.

Standish House
12 Myles Standish Hotel
Standish Shore
1871

In 1871, extensive plans were drawn up for a large cottage development and hotel. The Duxbury Shore Company was formed and land was purchased in an area now known as the Standish Shore. Major share holders included James Cook, William McAdams, and Cushing Webber. In 1872 a new road, Columbus Avenue (now Marshall Street), and a bridge were completed, giving access to all of this waterfront property.

The Standish House, Duxbury's first important watering place, opened its doors in July of 1871. Although located on Brewster property, the hotel was given the name Standish because that name was more prominent and because the Standish Monument stood on a bluff overlooking the shore where the hotel owned a half mile of beach.

Beginning as a relatively small building, the Standish House grew as its popularity spread. The *Old Colony Memorial*, April 11, 1872, carried the announcement: "the addition of two new wings will be ready for occupancy by July. The main building will be thrown into one large drawing room." Two years later, proprietor Charles C. Knapp added "fine new croquet grounds."

The cottage development proposed in 1871 never materialized, although individual summer houses, principally owned by share holders, were built. Several of these which are now winterized, still stand along Marshall Street.

The grounds were landscaped, and hammocks were strung up for afternoon siestas. There were floats, bath houses, and a new, 400-foot-long pier which was illuminated each evening. There were sailboats and rowboats for hire. Lawn tennis, a sport fast becoming popular with both men and women,

The Myles Standish Hotel at the turn of the century.

Advertisements
from the period.
(Anthony Kelso)

was available. An item from Ellis Harrison's scrapbook tells of an exciting event which delighted the guests. "Maurice Tappan of Brookline swam from 'Plum Hills' on Duxbury Beach to the hotel pier. . . a distance of five miles." This feat had never before been accomplished. The distance was covered in two hours and 30 minutes. Soon after, an advertisement stated: "No guest need have an idle moment."

The hotel offered every convenience. Many amenities such as hot and cold running water and electricity added immeasurably to everyone's comfort. The hotel's own post office was established in 1882, and ten years later a telephone was installed. The *Old Colony Memorial* reported: "Duxbury has been connected with the outside world by long distance telephone. The central office will be at the Hollis House and the Myles Standish Hotel." There was also a bicycle repair shop at the hotel, "for the worn out bicyclist who could find rest and refreshment, and where he could have either his raiment or wheel cleaned or repaired while preparing himself for the concert given nightly."

In 1877 when Samuel B. Beaman became the proprietor, the guest capacity of the hotel was 125. Guests could stay by the day for $3.00 or by the week from $18.00 to $30.00.

Many prominent people enjoyed visiting the Standish Shore. An item in the *Saturday Evening Gazette* of 1878 stated that the sporting facilities "are known to a large number of our most influential citizens who regularly pass the term in that vicinity."

John Kent, Sr. remembered an interesting hotel guest, Mr. Carl Pflueger, who spent most of the summer writing a musical comedy, "1492," and produced a couple of its numbers in the dance hall to entertain the guests. Girls and boys from the hotel and surrounding cottages performed "The Casino Girls" and "The Newsboys Chorus." John Kent's nine-year old voice was a fine soprano, and in his words, "The big boy wanted to take me to New York and give me a musical stage training." It is fortunate that Mr. Kent's mother took a dim view of this idea, for Mr. Pflueger soon ran into financial difficulties and was forced to sell "1492" to a promoter. After a short run, the "comedy died on the New York stage."

In 1890 when Francis A. Beyea and C. Win Perkins became the proprietors of the hotel, they changed the name to the Myles Standish Spring Hotel because of the wonderful spring on the property which provided the purest of waters. Mr. Beyea and Mr. Perkins may have lost a few patrons when they made "dressing for dinner" popular. Some guests who had spent many summers at the Old Standish House refused to return. Others, though, enjoyed the surroundings. Chinese rattan and wicker furniture graced the rooms and the spacious veranda. A barber shop was added, and for the first time golf was advertised, "the finest hotel golf-links in New England." The nine-hole course, 1754 yards long, was laid out behind the hotel. In order to join the Standish Golf Club one paid an initiation fee of $10.00 with annual dues of $25.00.

The hotel's heyday began in 1894, when L. Boyer and Sons of New York bought the property. They simplified the name to Myles Standish Hotel and

Standish Spring Bottling House

The spring on the property of the Standish House provided water "unequalled in softness and purity, second to none if not superior to any waters in the world and endorsed by the medical faculty and the public as absolutely pure and perfect, remarkable for its solvent properties."[15] This superior water, along with ginger ale and lemon soda, was commercially bottled in a house on the shore. Spanish labels have been found, evidence of widespread trade. The bottling house also served as an early headquarters for the Duxbury Yacht Club.

A nice bit of architectural ingenuity was used to make the spring itself considerably more attractive. The hotel owners surrounded it with enamel tiles and a peaked glass dome. Over all of this was erected a pergola with open sides, creating a charming area in which to have afternoon tea.

SPARKLING   NATURAL

MYLES STANDISH SPRING WATER.

PURE AND SOFT.

Sodium Chloride,	1,589 Grains
Sodic Sulphate,	0.077 "
Calcic Carbonate,	0.862 "
Magnesia Sulphate,	0.046 "
Oxide of Iron and Alumina,	0.031 "
Silica,	0.294 "
Organics,	Trace
Total,	2.899 "

retained Mr. Frank H. Palmer as manager. Bostonians had summered at the Standish House for years; now prosperous New Yorkers came too.

Most guests came by train. The Standish Express, at $1.25 roundtrip from Boston, brought visitors three times each day. The guests were met at the South Duxbury station by a carriage from the hotel. Other visitors came by boat from Plymouth and Boston.

The new owners advertised, "After having enjoyed your bath and sail, you will feel inclined to enter our spacious dining room and partake of soft clams served in the various forms, for which THE MYLES STAN-DISH is famous . . . It is, in fact, our constant endeavor to make our cuisine of the highest order, all of the appointments refined and homelike. The Boyers actually leased flats from the town and seeded them with clams so they would have a plentiful supply. A farm off Standish Street, owned by Jabez Griggs, supplied the hotel with fresh vegetables, milk, and eggs. Meals were served in the hotel dining room on English bone china.

Although he may not have been a guest at the hotel, John J. Enneking painted *The Duxbury Clam Diggers* nearby. Thomas Lawson, the financier known as the "copper king," summered at the Myles Standish. His grandson said that Lawson gave considerable thought to building his "Dreamwold" here for his beloved wife, but he chose Scituate instead after being rebuffed in his attempts to persuade the town of Duxbury to change its name to "Lawson."

There were two cannons on the spacious lawn leading to the water. One was regularly shot off at sunset. The cannon shot may have signaled the end of the day, but more gaiety awaited guests in the evening. There were nightly concerts and weekly dances. The masquerade balls were eagerly anticipated. There were

---

Wadsworth Family Reunion

On September 13, 1882 over 250 Wadsworth descendents, representing 19 different states and territories, had a reunion at the Myles Standish Hotel. Horace A. Wadsworth wrote in the family history of 1883: "Standish Shore assumed a gala-day appearance. Flags were displayed and over the main entrance was placed a large motto in evergreen bearing the name Wadsworth."

Guests included the Hon. Llewellyn A. Wadsworth of Hiram, Maine, James Wadsworth, the philanthropist, of Geneseo, New York, and a number of clergy and doctors. Many speeches were made and letters were read from those who were unable to attend. An excerpt from just such a letter from a Canfield, Ohio lady is worth sharing. "It is my opinion, that if people thought less of going to heaven, in some dim and far off future, and more of making one, and getting themselves into heavenly conditions just now, the world would get by such means a grander impetus that it ever had before."

prizes, such as opera glasses for the ladies and silver steins for the gentlemen. One sought-after souvenir presented to the ladies on certain occasions was a lovely silk fan imprinted with a picture of the hotel.

According to Miss Doris Beal, whose family summered on "The Ridge," Standish Shore's social life centered around the hotel. She would watch with fascination as her mother, dressing for a dance, would dip her curling iron down the globe of a kerosene lamp to heat it. Doris stayed awake at night to listen to the music which came wafting through the trees.

A social item from a Boston paper stated:

SOUTH DUXBURY, AUGUST 26 (probably 1896): A cake walk wound up another delightful week. The cake, huge and lavishly frosted, occupied a place of honor in the ballroom and whenever a contestant glanced in its direction his efforts were redoubled, for the cake was certainly worth winning. There was some very fancy stepping, singly and in pairs, and everyone was kept in continuous gales of laughter.

In 1898 a terrible storm carried away the Marshall Street bridge, severely damaging the hotel wharf and the bottling works. Although the damage was repaired, the bottling plant closed in 1905 because it was no longer profitable. The unique spring house gradually collapsed and the spring was capped for protection.

In July 12, 1908, a terrifying fire broke out at 11 p.m. when most of the guests were asleep. The local paper gave the following account:

HOTEL BARELY SAVED

MYLES STANDISH IN DANGER FROM FIRE WHICH DESTROYED STABLES

An opportune change of wind was all that saved the exclusive Myles Standish Hotel from complete destruction late tonight . . . the fire started in the

The hotel had its own post office.   (Arthur E. Beane)

garage about 30 feet from the hotel...Most of the guests had retired for the night and awoke to find their rooms filled with smoke. There was near panic . . . when the wind changed. The cause is thought to be spontaneous.

Miss Doris Beal recalls the fire vividly, although she was only four. She remembers being terrified by the flames and sparks. Certain that the fire would sweep the shore, the authorities told the residents to evacuate their homes. Doris' father warned her to sit on one of the trunks which had been packed and moved outside, and told her "not to move." He and her two older brothers joined a bucket brigade bringing water from a nearby pond. The town fire department and the bucket brigade, with the help of the change in wind direction, finally succeeded in putting out the fire.

Following these two natural misfortunes, the once-famous hotel started to decline. The resort depended on long-term guests, but cars now made it possible for guests to come just for a weekend. The hotel finally closed its doors in 1912 and stood shuttered and idle. After some pilfering occurred the owner suggested

The Brewer House was originally the north wing of the Standish Hotel.   (Fran Nichols)

The Adams House was originally the south wing of the Standish Hotel.   (Fran Nichols)

that some summer people had been supplying their cottages with hotel furniture and crockery.

Although the main hotel remained closed, the little bottling house was a center of activity during World War I. Civic-minded and capable, Mrs. Parker Whittington organized a group of ladies and their children to roll bandages in the house. The little girls knitted squares for afghans for soldiers. They would attach their names and some received letters from France from grateful soldiers.

After the Boyers defaulted on their mortgage, George G. Gregory took possession of the hotel in 1912. He eventually sold the parcel of land containing the hotel to E. Avery Brewer and William Orrell, brothers-in-law, with local realtor Percy Walker handling the transaction.

Brewer and Orrell decided to convert the hotel to private use. The rear and center portions were razed, but the north and south wings were preserved. Each wing, on its original site, became a separate house.

After Mr. Orrell's death in 1940, the south-wing half of the hotel was moved to the corner of Bradford Road and Marshall Street, and became the home of Mrs. Elinor Carter Lord, a long-time Standish Shore resident. It was appropriate that Mrs. Lord lived in part of the hotel as she and her sisters had often danced there. Later Fanueil Adams moved this house to 286 Marshall Street.

The house which had once been the north wing of the hotel remained on its original site at 262 Marshall Street. This house stayed in the Brewer family and has changed very little since the original renovation. Even the small door at the back entrance where ice was delivered directly into the cold storage area is still there.

Each of these Marshall Street houses retains a number of similarities attesting to the fact that both were once part of Duxbury's singularly grand hotel.

Winsor Hotel • Brunswick House • Bayside Inn

13 466 Washington Street
Seth Sprague, Jr.
1813

An item from the *Old Colony Memorial* dated April 11, 1872 announced, "Mr. Hollis, ex-state constable has purchased the fine old mansion . . .which is to be converted into a hotel and opened for the coming season. It will be run in connection with the 'popular house' of his father-in-law, George Paine Esq."[16] Mr. Hollis advertised, "The location is unexceptional, convenient to all points and unequaled in a first class hotel." Mr. Hollis was married to Gertrude Prior, daughter of Captain George Prior. An only child, Gertrude had as good a head for business as her husband, so her father was a generous backer of his son-in-law's undertakings.

By 1879 the house had been sold to John T. Winsor and was named the Winsor Hotel. By 1889 there was another new owner, the Honorable Joseph O. Burdett from Hingham. Five years later Mrs. F.V. Hunt was proprietor and the Winsor Hotel had become the Brunswick House. Rates were $1.50 per day. Part of the operation was a livery stable run by Fred Hunt.

Maurice Chandler acquired the property in 1912, either winning it or by legitimate purchase; no one is quite certain! During his tenure, a small house next to the livery stable was used for gambling. Eddie Loring is certain of this, for as he says, "I was one of the gamblers!" Mr. Chandler proceeded with many excellent changes. He cut a new door into the east side of the hotel facing Washington Street and added a large piazza enclosed with a decorative railing on two sides of the house. Over this railing Mrs. Chandler displayed her lovely hooked rugs for sale.

The hotel, renamed the Bayside Inn in 1912, remained in business until 1923. When the building was

The Seth Sprague, Jr. House, showing the new door on the Washington Street side and the piazza with decorative railing. The original front door faced Harrison Street.

Seth Sprague Jr.'s mansion became the Winsor Hotel in 1872. (Fran Nichols)

An advertisement for the Brunswick House.

converted into apartments in 1960, the railing was stored in the barn. Now it enhances the offices of the Duxbury Thrift Shop at the southwest end of Washington Street.

The house has several interesting architectural details. Willard deLue mentioned the unusual square enclosure on the roof, called a monitor.[17] This was used to illuminate and ventilate the upper story bedrooms. Just below the eaves there is a thick cable carved in wood, a reminder of the local shipping industry. What a privilege it must have been for summer guests to stay in such a beautiful inn!

In 1981 the apartments were converted into 7 condominiums under the aegis of Snug Harbor Condo Trust.

Hollis House • King's Hotel • Duxbury Inn

14 6 Fort Hill Lane
Levi Sampson, Sr.
c. 1811

The lovely, large house on the corner of Fort Hill Lane and Washington Street was built by Levi Sampson, Sr. for his son, Levi, Jr. It is difficult to date the house accurately. The earliest known date of construction is 1811, but Mr. Oliver Barker, an architect commissioned by Mrs. Marshall Dwinnell to help restore the house, noted many similarities to houses built earlier. He discovered that there were really two buildings involved. The original part of the house could have been built in the mid-eighteenth century and the ell, almost a century later.

Captain George C. Prior, a master mariner, and Gertrude W. Hollis, his daughter, owned the house in 1876. Later Gertrude and her husband, John, operated an inn there.

On the 1879 Duxbury Village map the house is called the "Captain George C. Prior House – Hollis Hotel." From an item in the *Duxbury Pilgrim* dated February 4, 1884, we learn, "Mr. C.F. Moore, a veteran hotel proprietor has charge of the Hollis House for the winter. Mr. Hollis is in town but part of the year and is very fortunate in securing the services of an experienced man like Mr. Moore." Only a few inns like the Hollis House were open year-round, so business must have been reasonably good. Mr. Hollis sold the hotel in 1893.

That same year, Mr. Charles T. Price, formerly of the Somerset Club and The Bachelor Quarters, Boston, became the proprietor. An ad in the 1894 *Duxbury Directory* lures guests by stating, "(This inn) has every

A fine pencil drawing (left) of this inn that changed its name three times, drawn when it was the King's Hotel and (right) as it stands today. (Fran Nichols)

Rumsellers and the Law

In the 1887–1888 Town Report the following
statement was printed:

"... there was no expenditure for sup-
pressing the illegal sale of liquor. However,
'but as the rumsellers' ways are so devious,
have not ... been able to gain evidence
sufficient to warrant an arrest but consider it
to be merely a question of time."

Along with liquor licenses, billiard and
pool licenses were also issued.

Duxbury Pool Room, 1910.

facility for Bathing, Boating, Gunning and Fishing."

In 1897 Mr. George W. King became manager and
the inn was called King's Hotel. His ad ran, "King's
Hotel. Near to all Points of Interest. Splendid Location. Comfortable rooms, overlooking Duxbury Bay."

On November 27, 1898 there was a violent storm
in Duxbury. An account in the *Old Colony Memorial*
stated, "At King's Hotel the roof of the barn was blown
off and great patches of shingles torn off the main
building . . .Henry Briggs' livery stable (north of the
hotel) was the scene of much excitement. (As) Briggs
led two horses up to King's Hotel . . .the roof blew off
knocking one of the horses down."[18]

In 1903 the property was purchased by Earl Summer. The inn, now called Duxbury Inn, was run by Mr.
B.A. Gilbert. Rooms were $2.00 per day and there were
accommodations for 30 guests.

In 1906 Maurice Chandler, Duxbury's colorful
entrepreneur, became proprietor of the inn. As the
story goes, he was a pretty sharp gambler from Cape
Cod whose specialty was a kind of shell game called
Props. Under Mr. Chandler's management the Duxbury
Inn was redecorated and refurnished. He advertised,
"A share of the Patronage of the Public is respectfully
solicited." During this period Duxbury was a dry
town, but liquor was brought into the inn by means of
a hidden staircase behind a chimney. The inn also had
a poolroom, and it was rumored that gambling took
place there as well.

By 1916 the property reverted to a private residence when Mr. Clifton Dwinnell purchased the house.
He received a letter from a lady who had lost a silver
chain while staying at the inn a decade earlier. When
the house was being renovated, workmen found the
chain, which was promptly returned to a very surprised but happy owner. Mr. Dwinnell would be
delighted to know that his granddaughter Carol and
her husband Thomas F. Burgess are now living in his
home, this property having remained in the same
family for the past 70 years.

St. George House •
Way Croft Inn
15 576 Washington Street

The St. George House was a small, popular inn on the corner of Washington and Sunset streets. (Robert Dente)

In the mid-1800s John Delano found manual employment in Duxbury for his friend George Scott. Being a careful and conscientious worker, Mr. Scott prospered. In 1890 he purchased a house on the southwest corner of Washington Street and Sunset Road for $3000 becoming one of the few black homeowners at the time.

George Scott and his wife Louise opened an inn and restaurant known as the St. George House. They advertised in the booklet, *The Pilgrim Town of Duxbury*, "Meals served at all hours." Mrs. Scott was certainly kept busy in the basement kitchen, as was her daughter, Maud, who helped wait on tables. John Delano's granddaughter, Mrs. Frank Dwyer, was 14 when she knew the Scotts. She was delighted with her new

The house as the Way Croft Inn. (Robert Dente)

friends and visited them regularly. She considered it a privilege when she was allowed to help Maud set the tables.

On March 8, 1895 the third meeting of the Duxbury Yacht Club was held at the St. George House. "The Charter having been received, permanent officers were elected."

In the 1903 Stage Coach Timetable rates for the St. George House are given, "$2.00 per day – $6.00–$8.00 per week. Capacity 30 people." As the house is not large, 30 people would appear to be more than it could accommodate. Mr. Scott's standards for his hostelry were high and it was very popular. He wrote a lengthy poem promoting his restaurant. What it lacks in meter and rhyme is made up for in sincerity.

In 1926 William T. Way bought the property for $8000. He continued to operate the inn on the site changing its name to Way Croft. Architects Adden and Parker were retained to draw up plans for a necessary addition. The stable for the inn, to the rear off Sunset Road, was remodeled into a lovely house for Maud Scott. Her mother, an invalid in her later years, eventually made her home with her daughter.

The house today. (Fran Nichols)

SOMETHING NEW

1. In good old Duxbury Town
    A Store has been started with Fair Renown.
    Many people have oftimes said: 'I wish in this Town
    a good Restaurant could be had'

2. Well, at last we have one, good and true,
    If you deal squarely with us, we will with you,
    We keep every-thing that is wanted, so come and buy,
    To please you well, the best we'll try.

3. We have Fruit, in tin cans no longer you will find,
    But in glass jars you will find all kinds,
    Home made Cake, Bread and Pie,
    I hope no one will pass us by.

4. If you are tired and hungry just come and see
    If you don't like our sandwiches we will give you coffee or Tea.
    A good Beef-steak or Mutton Chop you will soon see.
    Board and Lodging by the week or day.

5. When warm weather comes we will have Ice-cream
    Cool and refreshing to you it will seem.
    Everything in our store is neat and sweet,
    By another restaurant it cannot be beat.

6. Clam Chowder you will always find.
    Duxbury Clams are the best kind.
    If you come once, you will come again,
    You will always find us the same.

7. You will have no trouble to find our store,
    It is not far from the corner, a step or more.
    On Washington Street is where we are,
    Close by the Post Office and not far from the Hall.

GEO. W. SCOTT, CATERER

Powder Point Hotel

16 Corner of King Caesar and Weston Roads

1886

Across the bay from the Myles Standish Hotel, on Powder Point, another hotel with cottages opened its doors to guests in 1896. The hotel's main building, Powder Point Hall, and auxiliary cottages belonged to the Powder Point School, which opened in 1886. These buildings were designed by the Headmaster Frederick B. Knapp, an MIT graduate and an excellent mathematician. Mr. Knapp bought the 15-16 acre property, which included the King Caesar House, from the heirs of Ezra Weston, Jr. There was ample space for the school's playing fields, tennis courts, and even a golf course.

The Powder Point School's location was so beautiful that the buildings were put to use during the students' summer vacation as well. The cell-like size of the dormitory rooms, however, prompted Mrs. Helen Howe to comment: "They should have been ashamed to take any money for them." But the beauty of Duxbury lured many families from their spacious Boston homes to summer at the hotel year after year. One write-up captured the setting, "The situation is one of the most attractive on the South Shore . . .and commands a beautiful land and sea view which includes the village, the bay, Gurnet Lights and Plymouth in the distance."[19] Other campus buildings served the summer guests as well. "The Cottage," which still stands at 126 King Caesar Road, was a faculty house during the school year and provided sleeping rooms for the summer hotel guests. "The Cottage" is now owned by Mrs. Laurence Hunter. The school laboratory doubled as a parlor for the visitors.

The Powder Point Hotel boasted of seashore and country advantages in this advertisement.

Another building was named "The Grove" because it was in a lovely grove of trees called "Circle of Thorn Trees" by Ezra Weston IV, a gentleman horticulturalist. Virginia Ludwig remembered the ladies rushing out after luncheon, vying for the hammocks with the best views. This building was eventually torn down.

Mr. C.M. Reade was manager of the Powder Point Hotel in 1896. Dr. John D. Adams wrote in a 1951 *Duxbury Clipper*, "He directed it with a firm and strict discipline." The hotel could accommodate 90 guests at a cost of $2.00 per day each. The food was excellent and it was enjoyed in relative serenity, as there was a special dining room for children and their nurses. The large school bell rang to announce meal times. Occasionally the smaller children were allowed to ring it, some having to jump very high in order to reach the rope. Mr. Reade also arranged for regular clambakes each summer.

Powder Point School for boys made a fine summer hotel after students left on summer vacations.

Mr. and Mrs. Paul Courtney along with their children were guests at the hotel each year beginning in 1916. Mrs. Courtney was particularly fond of young people. According to Mrs. Roderic MacDonald, she would put on marvelous parties in the gym. Everyone would play charades and there were always costume parties. Mrs. MacDonald remembers her mother dressing her as an angel when she was about thirteen, and in her own words, "perfectly square. I was mortified."

Traveling Armenian peddlers would arrive at the hotel each summer with their fancy linens, displaying them for the guests to enjoy and purchase.

School was in session on May 13, 1913 when a fire broke out. Masters and boys fought valiantly, but the water supply gave out and the main building was reduced to ashes. By July another building was being erected, but it was necessary for the hotel to find other accommodations for summer patrons. The hotel leased 138 Powder Point Avenue from Mr. Eben Ellison where they served meals.

World War I marked the end of many smaller private schools. In 1926 when the Powder Point School closed its doors, the hotel closed as well. In 1930 Powder Point Hall was purchased by the National Sailor's Home of Massachusetts. (The other buildings were remodeled into private residences.) This seaside location for retired Naval personnel appeared to have been ideal, but with no public transportation the men were lonely and had very little to occupy their time. Once again the building was closed in 1974.

That same year a group of men formed the Powder Point Realty Trust and purchased the property. After considerable research, they decided to raze the building. This was accomplished reluctantly for it is not easy to demolish a landmark that, in its day, resounded with the laughter of both the young and old.

The Franklin House •
The Colonial Inn

17 470 Washington Street

Nathaniel Winsor Jr.

1807

The four handsome houses at the juncture of Harrison Street, Washington Street, and Mattakeesett Court form Duxbury's most elegant corner. The stately federal house on the southeast corner was built by Nathaniel Winsor, Jr. in 1807. The builder's fine craftsmanship is evident outside and in. Much of the interior woodwork, particularly the inlay in the mantelpiece in the front hall, was carved by Mr. Winsor, who also carved ships' figureheads. It is possible that he had a hand in carving the over-mantel mirror as well. The beautiful spiral staircase, said to be modeled after a Bulfinch design, rises two flights. Legend has it that

A post card of the Colonial Inn.   (Mildred Glass)

The Nathaniel Winsor, Jr. House has had many interesting guests. (Fran Nichols)

27

The beautiful spiral staircase which rises two flights.

ships' masts were actually made in the house in this deep stairwell. In the winter months seamen worked on the masts during the day and slept at night in hammocks hung from the third-floor rafters.

In 1903 the Nathaniel Winsor house, called The Franklin House, was open year-round to guests. Run by Messrs. Hannigan and Kane, it was a trifle more expensive than other guest houses in the immediate area. Accommodations cost $2.00 per day, or $7.00 to $10.00 by the week.

Mr. Maurice Chandler purchased the property in 1916, for $7000, and renamed it The Colonial Inn. The 1916 graduating class of Partridge Academy held their dinner there. A member of this class, Mrs. Helen Howe, said she and her fellow classmates felt very grown-up and sophisticated, never having been in a hotel before.

The Nathaniel Winsor, Jr. house was privately owned during the 1930s and 1940s. In 1949 Dr. and Mrs. Edwin Leonard purchased this beautiful property, and it remains in the family today. When Dr. Leonard was forced into retirement after a heart attack, the Leonards decided to share their house with guests once again. The Doctor became famous for his gourmet breakfasts. A peek at the guest book conjures up images of thought-provoking after-dinner conversations, for guests ranged from Buckminster Fuller, inventor of the geodesic dome, to Sir William Hawthorne, Master of Churchill College, Cambridge, to Margaret Hamilton, best known as the Wicked Witch of the West in the movie *The Wizard of Oz*.

Many people have enjoyed the hospitality of this early nineteenth-century house, where a suit of armor affectionately named "Sir Anthony" (after an English ancestor) guards the door. Who will ever forget the glorious sight of glowing candlelight in each and every window during the Christmas season?

The Hill Crest Inn

18 60 Crescent Street

c. 1910

Mrs. Nelson Smith, known as "Aunt Smith," acquired some property in 1910 from J. Mercer Seaver, an elderly gentleman whom she had befriended and cared for over a period of years. Mr. and Mrs. Smith built the Hill Crest Inn and then ran it with their three children, Annie, Blanche, and Walter. As his parents grew older, Walter assumed the responsibility of management.

Like many summer cottages, the Inn had a wrap-around veranda which took advantage of a panoramic sea view. A huge fireplace made of quartz dominated the parlor. The downstairs rooms and porch were furnished with wicker and oak. There were only seven or eight bedrooms at the Hill Crest Inn, but there was space in the large dining room for extra diners who might be treated to succulent lobsters and vegetables from the nearby garden.

The Fusilier Veterans Association celebrated its 133rd Anniversary in May, 1920 by dining at the Hill Crest Inn. A few years later the members of the Mount Tabor Masonic Lodge were treated to a shore dinner that included a wide variety of seafood. If anyone still suffered pangs of hunger, there was chicken "with all the fixin's." The cost of this extraordinary outing, including a round trip bus ticket from Boston, was $3.25. An advertisement for the Hill Crest Inn stated that "this business of Diogenes looking for an honest man with his lantern was nonsense. What Diogenes was looking for, really was chicken and waffles. Chicken, tender as a maiden's heart and cooked to a delicate golden brown in heavenly, homemade butter. Waffles, light as a fairy's dance—melting as a lover's glance—nestling in ambrosian syrup." Nelson Ferrell, Nelson Smith's namesake, remembers that Mr. Ben Dawes, custodian of the Myles Standish Monu-

Guests enjoying the view of Kingston Bay at the Hill Crest Inn in South Duxbury. (Robert Dente)

Interior of Hill Crest with the quartz fireplace. (Eli Solomon)

ment, was a permanent summer boarder at the Hill Crest Inn. He also said his Uncle Walter was known as "am I busy Smith," for besides running the inn, he also had a thriving shellfish business that supplied the best restaurants. Boats full of fish were winched up to a small building on the property close by the water, where the fish were cleaned and made ready for shipment. Some Fridays some fish never did get cleaned, so the building was soon dubbed "the maggot house." There was also a blacksmith shop on the inn property, where Nelson fashioned superior clamdiggers on his forge.

The inn closed in the early 1930s, but Mrs. Dorothy Wentworth, Duxbury's town historian for 35 years, was persuaded to reopen it in 1938. Her husband had worked there as a boy and had continued his friendship with Walter Smith. Mrs. Wentworth put in one working summer and broke even. "I was young, willing, and confident," she recalled, "but innkeeping was not to my liking." The hotel was finally closed in 1939.

View of the house today. (Fran Nichols)

Standard Fertilizer Company

In 1882, long before the Hill Crest Inn was built, the property was the site of the Standard Fertilizer Company. This company was a major industry in Duxbury where the pogys or menhaden that were abundant along the Atlantic Coast were converted into fertilizer and oil. This caused considerable concern to nearby residents. Petitions appeared in the town warrant requesting the factory be shut down, stating, "the existing smell had ill effects on the weaker sex."[20] However, the State Board of Health, Lunacy and Charity ruled a "smell in itself was in no way injurious to one's health."[21] And so the company remained in business.

Eagle Tree Inn
19   157 Washington Street
1893

In 1893 Fanny Davenport MacDowell built a large house overlooking the bay which she called "Melbourne Hall." Although the estate has been greatly modified and altered over the years, if one walks around the exterior with a picture of the original house in hand, one can still visualize the "manor house." A pamphlet called the architecture a "happy combination of Norman and Dutch effects." The 13-acre waterfront property had its own private pier where Fanny's husband, W. Melbourne MacDowell, kept his yacht, the "Fanny D." He was the first commodore of the Duxbury Yacht Club.

Fanny Davenport MacDowell was a well-known actress who made her stage debut at the age of ten. Probably her most famous part was Cleopatra in the play of the same name.

Interior of the Eagle Tree Inn.   *(Robert A. Hutchinson)*

A circular drive leading off Washington Street wound its way to Melbourne Hall, which later became the Eagle Tree Inn. (Raymond Day, Jr. and Nell Day Hamilton)

The house today.   (Fran Nichols)

In the 1920s Melbourne Hall became the Eagle Tree Inn. As the main part of the house had five very large bedrooms and the servants quarters four more, it was well suited to accommodate summer guests. The entrance hall had panels of stained glass showing Arab scenes adapted from the paintings done by Schreyer. First-time guests must have paused and wondered if they really were in Duxbury.

Mrs. John E. Andresen's grandparents stayed there, as did Mrs. Virginia Ludwig with her parents. Helen Eaton and her family occupied most of the house at one time. Her parents, an aunt, a sister with her husband, two children, a nurse and a personal maid were joined on weekends by her brother and his wife. They found the Eagle Tree a fine place in which to relax. On rainy days the youngsters had a marvelous time exploring its numerous hideaways.

Later the Eagle Tree Inn became Mrs. George Putnam Metcalf's private home, called "Westwinds by the Sea." Mrs. Metcalf opened Westwinds Book Shop, precursor of the present bookstore, in the carriage house of the estate.

At the east end of Island Creek Pond was a family camp, Cushing's Grove.   (Russell Edwards, Fanny Hathaway and Nettie Edwards)

An area off Tobey Garden Street at the east end of Island Creek Pond was once bustling with activity. Benjamin Cushing owned a considerable amount of land around the pond which his brothers, Winslow and Walter, inherited in the nineteenth century. Winslow decided to clear part of the area for a small park, calling it Cushing's Grove.

The Grove was simple and rustic. There was a cabin in which one could play pool and in another homemade ice cream and lemonade were available, which was, of course, popular with the children. There was a covered dance floor near the water for parties, and boats were provided for added pleasure.

In 1911 a few cottages were built in the area for families who came to Duxbury for the summer. These could be rented by the week or month for $1.00 per day including a boat. The dance floor was deemed expendable, so the first cabin was erected from these old floor boards. Mrs. Fanny Hathaway and her sister Mrs. Nettie Edwards recall a wonderful summer spent in this cabin while their mother, Mrs. Ida Cushing Holman, was recovering from tuberculosis. Everything was primitive. However, Mother Nature, in her inimitable way, bordered the paths to the outhouse with honeysuckle which made the walk, according to Mrs. Edwards, rather pleasurable.

In 1928 Winslow Cushing sold the park to a syndicate. It was now called Tinkertown Acres and managed by Rodman and Goldman. The new owners added a small beach and built a large pavilion which dominated the water's edge and was used for various functions. A bit later Lawrence (Buck) Freeman ran

Members of the Rebekahs "Helping Hand" c.1915 at Cushing's Grove including Ella Hodgdon, Clara McNaught and her sister, Myrtie Soule, Lucy Morrison, Marian Wilder, Jennie Glover, Clara Shirley, and Nancy Gloves. (Russell Edwards)

the park for about four years. On Sundays the guests would go over to the Sweetheart Tearoom on Tremont Street to enjoy the specialty, golden waffles.

After the town of Duxbury denied Tinkertown Acres a liquor license, the property was sold to Mr. O.B. Brown who ran a camp for underprivileged black children. Eventually it became more of a musical society named Four Clovers and run by Mr. John Woodbury and a Mr. Hayes. There were weekly concerts in the pavilion and stage performances too, for trunks full of costumes were later found. Guests also enjoyed expeditions to Duxbury Beach.

It is rumored that the camp may have served as a depot for contraband liquor during Prohibition. Being secluded, it was also suspected of having been a nudist colony.

As late as 1946 the pavilion still stood. Priscilla Wentworth Sheeley remembers going there with her Girl Scout troop to perform in plays for a badge. She said that the girls' voices echoed all around the big hall in a delightfully scary way. Since this area is now all residential, it is difficult to visualize the camp, but some say the pavilion foundation can still be found off Island Creek Road.

Myles Manor Inn

21 90 Standish Street

Dr. Ira Chandler

1872

In 1925 the house was owned by George E. and H.J. Farrington. They rented it to Mr. and Mrs. Paul McKenney who ran it as the Myles Manor Inn.

Most local people recall the barn, rather than the inn, because its hardwood floor, balcony, and small rooms around the perimeter made it an ideal place for dancing. The barn at that time was attached to the south side of the house. Johnny Slater's "Crimson Ramblers" provided the music. Mr. Larry McCarthy of Pill Hill Lane recalls filling in at the piano when the regular pianist was unavailable. There was tea dancing each Saturday afternoon. Mrs. Edwin Noyes, Mrs. Virginia Ludwig, and Mrs. Russell Seaver all had happy memories of the Duxbury spot, where the music was delightful.

The Standish Shore Association often hired the barn for private parties, where Miss Doris Beal happily "danced her feet off." While a student at Wheelock College, she also ran a kindergarten in this building during the summer of 1923.

There are those who say the barn was also a speakeasy at one time. Dr. Ira Chandler would have enjoyed his house being used in this way, for he relished a fast-paced life. The doctor would harness his frisky horse to the rubber-tired buggy in the barn with all doors firmly shut; then, with the reins wrapped around his wrists, he would tell his wife, Louise, to "open up." The horse would take the bit and run at top speed until he reached the railroad crossing on Depot Street, almost a mile away. Needless to say, everyone scattered when they saw this buggy coming. Doctor Chandler may not have imbibed spirits, but he certainly was spirited!

Damaged by fires in 1983 and 1984, Dr. Chandler's house has been carefully renovated by Jorgen S. Nielsen, the current owner.

A fine dance hall in the large barn was an attraction at the Myles Manor Inn on Standish Street. (Russell Edwards)

Shore Acres Inn

22   333 Tremont Street

c. 1824

Louise Chandler and her husband, Norman St. George, opened the Shore Acres Inn in the late 1920s in the house that had been in her father's family since 1825. The owners advertised, "Famous Duxbury Clams a Specialty." A phrase attributed to Elder Brewster describes these mollusks as "treasures hid in the sand." Shore Acres Inn chefs obviously found their hiding places too.

After Norman St. George died, Louise married Carl Stowe, an actor. Together they continued to run the inn, and because of Mr. Stowe's theatrical background, they attracted other thespians. Among the well-known guests were Flo and May Irwin who popularized ragtime in vaudeville.

Local residents remember that Mrs. Stowe cut quite a figure in her striking outfits, with white gloves and the huge cartwheel hat she wore when doing her daily shopping.

Shore Acres Inn was especially popular with actors and actresses.   (Top: Robert Dente, bottom: Fran Nichols)

The house across Soule Avenue at 347 Tremont Street was a necessary adjunct to Shore Acres, as the waitresses and other help stayed there. The house has been very attractively renovated.   (Fran Nichols)

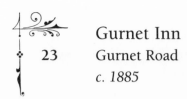

Gurnet Inn

23　Gurnet Road

c. 1885

The original Gurnet Inn, a 16–18 room structure, was built in 1752.[22] Located near Gurnet Light in Plymouth, this inn was reached by ox cart from Green Harbor along the sandy shore of Duxbury beach. It was in operation from 1860 to about 1920. Some time during the 1920s the building burned down.

The "new" Gurnet Inn was opened in 1927, a year after Mrs. Mary Quinn purchased an 1885 house and land on the Gurnet Road in the Duxbury Beach area. Mrs. Quinn and her daughter Mary, Mrs. Frank Cosgrove, began with a tearoom where they served a delicious high tea. They soon enlarged their business, first renting rooms, and then opening a restaurant. The inn became so popular that Mrs. Quinn hired help from North Carolina, where the Frank Cosgroves were managers of the Pinehurst Country Club.

The whole family worked together in Duxbury, just as they did in the South. Mrs. Cosgrove's daughters, Jean and Louise, waited on table and Mrs. Quinn and Mrs. Cosgrove did most of the cooking.

A third Cosgrove daughter, Ann, better known as "Buttons," was an outstanding golfer and the Massachusetts State titlist in 1950. She married another champion golfer, Julius Boros, who became a well-

Left: The Gurnet Inn as it appeared around 1930. (Jean Stevenson)
Above: The inn as it looks today. (Fran Nichols)

known tour professional. Tragedy struck a year or so later when Mrs. Boros died in childbirth. The Ann Cosgrove Boros golf tournament, played on the South Shore every year, was started by her sister and mother in her memory.

After the death of her daughter Ann, Mrs. Cosgrove lost interest in the inn. She turned it over to her daughter Louise and son-in-law Wilfred Weldon, who ran it from 1952 to 1957. During this period the inn was changed into eight housekeeping apartments.

In 1957 Jack Stevenson, Jean Cosgrove's husband, acquired the inn. He said, "I am a beach boy with sand in my shoes and cannot bear to be away too long from the shore."

The Gurnet Inn is a family vacation spot to which guests return year after year. One family from Bronxville, New York has been coming for twenty-four summers. The inn has a beautiful outlook of sea and sand, and each apartment has a water view. There is a cocktail lounge and a restaurant on the street side of the building. The inn opens on Memorial Day and closes in the middle of September.

Until the storm of 1898, there was enough beach for boys to play baseball. Once there was also a road that ran along the waterside in front of the inn, but the beachfront eroded. Time and tide made a seawall a necessity. During the blizzard of 1978 this seawall only partially protected the inn, which suffered $94,000 worth of damage. Mr. Stevenson's first thought was to bulldoze the whole structure and start again, but a wise contractor persuaded him that much could be saved. Since part of the Gurnet Inn is over 100 years old, it is fortunate that this comfortable and unpretentious summer hostelry has been preserved.

Interior of the Gurnet Inn. (Jean Stevenson)

Twin Oaks
24   West End of South Street

After the Four Clovers closed, John Woodbury worked with his brother-in-law at the Highway Hotel in Kingston, where the telephone company offices are now. In the 1930s Mr. Woodbury and his wife, Ella, opened a family camp called Twin Oaks which catered to blacks. The camp was at the west end of South Street on the Kingston border.

At Twin Oaks there was a main building which housed the dining room, with cabins to the right and left. There was also a swimming pool — quite a luxury for the time!

Mr. Woodbury came from Chicago, where, it is said, he drove for Al Capone. A gourmet chef, he and his wife, a former teacher and a graduate of Southern College for Women in Alabama, cooked for the guests at this very nice camp. Richard Schaffer remembered installing two hotel-sized iron ranges in the basement kitchen which was neatly and efficiently arranged with long work tables. Meals at Twin Oaks were elegant. Waitresses were dressed in black with carefully starched white aprons and caps. During the winter when Twin Oaks was closed, the Woodburys often catered to Duxbury parties.

Gertrude Coffin, who lives nearby, remembers Ella Woodbury well. Mrs. Coffin was grateful when the many Coffin children were invited for a swim in the Twin Oaks pool. There were plenty of cats around to delight the youngsters, who also enjoyed the ice cream cones which were sold at the camp. Mr. and Mrs. Woodbury were childless but loved children. Whenever her good friend, Mrs. Coffin, appeared with her brood for ice cream, Ella Woodbury would say, "Gertrude, aren't you going to leave me any babies today?"

Twin Oaks prospered for years. A great many professional guests, mostly doctors and lawyers, returned year after year. The property was sold in 1975 to a condominium developer.

Twin Oaks, a popular camp for professional families from New York City. (Robert Dente and Gertrude Coffin)

The Red Jacket Inn, across Bay Road from the Duxbury Playhouse was named for the clipper ship Red Jacket. (Fran Nichols)

The clipper ship Red Jacket by Currier and Ives, (Sotheby's, New York) and the sign for the inn. (Robert Dente)

Red Jacket Inn

25   170 Loring Road

1700s

Originally built, perhaps in the 1700s, as a small farmhouse, this property was purchased by Atherton Loring in the 1930s. He expanded the house using many different types of wood supplied by his lumber business.

By the 1940s the house was being run as an inn. Owner and manager Marion T. Baker loved the sea. The name *Red Jacket* was taken from a ship built by Mrs. Baker's great-grandfather, George Thomas, at Rockland, Maine in 1864 and depicted in a rare Currier & Ives lithograph. The Red Jacket Inn was a charming establishment. The gold and red tea chest paper used in the downstairs hall enhanced Mrs. Baker's extensive library on clipper ships.

The Duxbury Playhouse, which operated from the late 1940s until 1951, was located across the street from the Red Jacket Inn. A number of actors and actresses at the Playhouse who stayed at the inn went on to greater glory in Boston and New York theaters. John Cassavetes acted at the Playhouse and became a very famous movie director. Claudia MacNeil went directly from acting here to Broadway where she was in "Raisin in the Sun." In 1951 David Blair McCloskey, a well-known voice teacher and therapist, took over the Playhouse and it became the Plymouth Rock Center of Music and Drama. Here, opera singers were given the opportunity to further their musical ambitions.

By 1955 this small center for the arts had closed and Mrs. Baker decided to relocate in North Plymouth. The Red Jacket Inn is now a private residence.

Boarding Houses

It was not always easy for guests who were not residents of Duxbury to find accommodations in town. In 1774 the town voted to enact a law imposing a fine on all persons taking any boarders or visitors overnight from another town without notifying the selectmen as to where they came from and how long they were to stay. This was certainly a very early type of passport requirement.

Taverns throughout Duxbury welcomed travelers in the eighteenth century, but by the nineteenth century more permanent housing was needed for workers in the huge shipbuilding industry. Boarding houses provided such accommodations. These were generally private homes in which the boarder was provided a place to sleep and a chair at the family dining table for a weekly fee. The Charles Krahmer house at 18 Fort Hill Lane is purported to have boarded sailors. There was certainly plenty of room for them. The house boasts ten fireplaces so the young lads were undoubtedly more fortunate than others when the weather turned damp or cold. In addition to the shipyard workers, many other people commonly stayed in boarding houses in the early days, including shool teachers and railroad workers.

Toward the end of the nineteenth century there was a need for accommodations for a different type of guest, the summer visitor. In some of the old

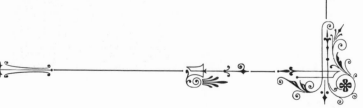

boarding houses shipwright boarders were replaced by summer people. Additional accommodations were also offered as some large old sea captains' houses were turned into boarding houses for seasonal guests.

Additional boarding houses in Duxbury between 1890 and 1915 included those run by Mrs. Donald McIntosh on Washington Street, Mrs. Louisa J. Symes and Mrs. Sheppard on Powder Point Avenue, and Mrs. Richmond on Washington Street, but to date there is little information on these establishments.

Recently tourists have been accommodated in bed-and-breakfasts in Duxbury homes. Each house echoes with the lives of former owners, and in a few their spirits have returned!

View of Washington Street taken in 1906.

Daniel Peterson
26   612 Washington Street
1804

Mr. Peterson was a mariner and a ship's carpenter. It is possible he built some of this house himself. In 1810 Reuben Drew purchased the property for $1400 to use as an adjunct to his flourishing Bluefish River shipyard. For the next 15 years this residence served as a boarding house for shipwrights, ropemakers, sailmakers, and the like. Mr. and Mrs. Frank B. Lawson, the present owners, are appreciative of the historic dimension their house played in the exciting shipbuilding era.

(Russell Edwards)

Launching Duxbury's Fleet

The launching of a ship in Duxbury was undoubtedly a gala occasion. If humanly possible, everyone attended this major event. Although high water determined the hour, the launching usually took place at 11:00 a.m. Joyful children were released from school as many of their fathers had a hand in the building of the ship.

Sometimes there was a road between the shipyard and the water, "so that at launching time ways had to be laid across the highway and teams were obliged to go through the yard and around the vessels on the stocks."[23] All of the hard work was worth it. One fortunate young lad was selected to stand on the vessel's bow-sprit holding by a short lanyard a bottle of wine or something of the sort, which he broke over the bow just as the vessel took to the water. This was called "dashing the bottle."[24] It was every youngster's dream to grow to be a man chosen for the occasion to perform this act.

An extra portion of grog would be issued to the workers who were justly proud of their craftsmanship. All along the shore people raised their mugs with cries of, "Success to this ship."

27   17 Stetson Place
James Woodward
1801

28   Judith Hathaway's House
Washington Street

In 1821 Andrew Stetson married Sylvia, daughter of Dr. and Mrs. Rufus Hathaway. Soon after, they opened their house to boarders. A young schoolmaster who was boarding there wrote the following verse.

> Let no one, who in Duxbury
> May happen to stop,
> Think he's seen all the sights
> Till he's seen Stetson's shop.[25]

Andrew Stetson was a village cordwainer. An amiable man, his shop on Main Street (now Washington Street) was a gathering place for people from all walks of life.

The shoemaker's house, which actually faces Bumblebee Lane, was surrounded by shrubbery called Bouncing Bets, which attracted so many bees that the lane was called "Bumblebee."

In the 1790s Rufus Hathaway and his wife Judith lived on Washington Street in the vicinity of 520 Washington Street. Rufus was a successful portrait painter and doctor, but his untimely death at age 52 was catastrophic for his young wife who was left with 11 children. To ease her financial situation, Judith boarded ships' carpenters and baked bread and cakes to sell to her neighbors.

A devastating fire consumed Judith Hathaway's house. As no records of fires were kept at that time, we do not know when this disaster occurred. She moved to 19 Chapel Street where she lived until her death at the age of 102.

Charles Stetson and his wife, Pauline, in front of his father, Andrew Stetson's house. (Left: Carolyn Ames, right: Fran Nichols)

Life of a Shipwright

The life of a shipworker, whether he was a carpenter, ropemaker, sailmaker, or forger, was rigorous and satisfying. Many workers could observe the fruition of their labors within sight of their homes. They toiled from sunup to sundown with two breaks during the day. It was the custom to serve grog at 11 a.m. and again at 4 p.m. At the shipyards all over Duxbury the ringing cry of 'Grog O' could be heard. All hands would "quit work, adjourn to the work-house and 'smiled.' "[26] The industry required ruggedness in their shipwrights. "It took rum to build ships in those days; a quart to a ton, by rough allowance; and more to launch her properly."[27]

Very often the master would work along with his men, and in the evenings they would gather together in the master's house. Around a roaring fire munching on apples and nuts and quaffing mugs of cider, the shipwrights would discuss tides and storms. Their talk turned spicy when an argument broke out, but most of the time it was a convivial gathering.

The late Hon. E.S. Tobey once said, "To speak of the character of the numerous first class ships which have been built here (Duxbury) would be to recall the names of the best mechanics and skilled artisans of the whole country."[28]

Shipwright

The Cottage By The Sea

29 4 Surplus Street
Benjamin Bosworth
1784

Another boarding house for shipwrights was in the area known in the 1700s as "Hell's Corner." Built in 1784 by Benjamin Bosworth, the house later was converted to a two-family house. In the late 1800s the owner, Mrs. Delano, took in summer boarders. The old latches, narrow stairs, and big fireplaces delighted her guests at "The Cottage by the Sea." In June, 1890 the Reverend Mr. Babcock from Baltimore summered here, transforming "Hell's Corner" into "Heavens Corner."[29] The house was long the residence of Mrs. W. Richmond Arnold who was the Society Editor for the Boston Herald for many years. In 1988–89 the house was greatly enlarged.

Shipwrights boarded at Benjamin Bosworth's 1784 house on the corner of Washington and Surplus streets. (Above: Russell Edwards, right: Fran Nichols)

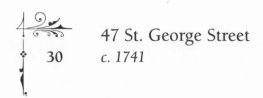

47 St. George Street
30 *c. 1741*

An English couple, Mr. and Mrs. Frank Howard, shared their large house and property on both sides of St. George Street with summer guests in the 1890s. The Howards were a talented family. For many years Mr. Howard was organist at King's Chapel in Boston, and he gave vocal lessons. The Howard's daughter gave piano lessons, and their son's paintings hung in the King Caesar House at one time.

The original part of the Howards' house was built circa 1741. An addition was later built to accommodate workers from Israel Sylvester's shipyard which was located directly in front of the house.

The house today.   (Fran Nichols)

Pictured at Riverlea in 1914 are Alice, Hope and Fred Potter along with their friend Bobby Osborne.   (Alice Hoyt)

2 Water Street

31　James Winsor
1796

Like so many other Duxbury widows, Mrs. Susan Wilde took in boarders at the end of the nineteenth century. Hortense Merry, Fire Chief, stayed at Mrs. Wilde's house. Her granddaughter, Myra Shepard Wadman, carried on the boarding house after Mrs. Wilde died. Myra was outspoken and considered a character, but very well-liked. She lived with many cats who were some of her best friends.

A fine example of a three-quarter Cape Cod house built by James Winsor. (Above: Fran Nichols, below: Dickie and Gillian Dillon)

Mudjekeewis

32 Formerly on the corner of Washington Street and Shipyard Lane

c. 1800

"Honor be to Mudjekeewis!" With a shout exclaimed the people, "Honor be to Mudjekeewis!" Henceforth he shall be the West Wind! And hereafter and forever. Shall he hold supreme dominion Over all the winds of heaven.

—Song of *Hiawatha* by H.W. Longfellow

On the corner of Washington Street and Shipyard Lane Mrs. D.A. Banister ran her simple boarding house called Mudjekeewis. She advertised "People of quiet tastes will find the house of Mrs. Banister a desirable one, combining country and sea-shore. Perfect sanitary arrangements, good beds, lawn pine grove, bathing house near—special rates for the season." An item about Mudjekeewis appeared in the August 26, 1898 issue of the *Old Colony Memorial* newspaper. "Yesterday a large party from Mudjekeewis cottage held a picnic and clam-bake on Saquish. On Monday evening there will be a dance for guests and their friends." The latter was presumedly held at the Standish Hotel. Later, after Mrs. Banister's became a private home, it was destroyed by fire. Another house has been built on the site and is now the home of Mr. and Mrs. Wilfred Sheehan.

Mrs. Banister's guests enjoying a lively spider-web party. (Raymond Day, Jr. and Nell Day Hamilton)

62 Washington Street
33 *1839*

Alden School
34 43 Cedar Street
1822

Mrs. Micah Soule operated a summer boarding house here in 1896. Architectural purists now delight in the lack of changes to the exterior of the house since its construction in 1839.

(Above: Mr. and Mrs. William Dixon, below: Fran Nichols)

Jonathan Smith, a sea captain who made many profitable voyages, built this fine colonial house in 1822.

Around the turn of the century, the house served different purposes throughout the year. Starting in 1896, during the winter it was the Alden School, a resident and day school for young ladies. The campus had tennis courts, croquet grounds, and "fine shade trees."[30] Helen Nevers, one of the principals, opened the house in the summer for boarders. She had the good business sense to utilize what the property offered, and her guests must have enjoyed the changing river scene and the wild birds attracted to the area.

The former Alden School.   (Fran Nichols)

122 Powder Point Avenue
35 Simeon Soule
c. 1800

During Duxbury's shipbuilding era many workers from the shipyards boarded here. Mrs Fergus Steele, who purchased the house in 1917, took in summer guests in the mid-1920s. Being close to the water and the outer beach, the property made an ideal spot for vacationers.

Mr. and Mrs. Paul Barber owned the house from 1955 to 1989. He was a Duxbury selectman for 9 years.

The property has recently been acquired by Proctor-Ellison Company.

The house today.   Fran Nichols)

Mrs. Fergus Steele took in summer boarders at her house on Powder Point Avenue. (Mr. and Mrs. Paul Barber)

Sally Joyce's

36   277 Washington Street
Ezra Prior
1800

In the early 1900s Sally Joyce operated a convenient and comfortable residence for year-round boarders. Cora Soule Robinson once wrote, "My mother boarded in the winter months for twelve years with Miss Sally Joyce. She was not pleased the Joyces seldom locked their doors when they went out, so she carried her spare money and her jewelry in a little homemade chamois bag wherever she went." Another winter guest was William Field, an actor, whose nearby summer home was unheated.

Mr. and Mrs. H. Dennison White, parents of Mrs. Edwin Noyes, lived across the street, and they often offered accommodations for extra boarders when the Joyce house was filled for the summer. Nellie Came, a boarder, true to her name, came and stayed with the Whites for four years. She ate her meals with the Joyces, but if upon her return to the White's house they were still enjoying corn on the cob, she was not averse to finishing every extra ear. This feat, of course, was anticipated.

The Joyce house faces a lane that once ran from Tremont Street to the shore. Sally's mother, Marm Joyce, was widowed young and ran a notions shop in one corner of her house. Here she sold needles, thread, and ribbons that she bought in Boston. To buy these goods, Marm Joyce sailed to the city on the Boston packet which she boarded at the end of the lane. She saved her good shoes from the morning dew by walking barefoot to the shore. Sally Joyce was also a seamstress, perhaps with a skill learned from her thrifty mother.

At left, guests enjoying a game of tennis at Sally Joyce's boarding house. (Mr. and Mrs. Timothy Leland); below the house today.   *(Fran Nichols)*

Sally B. Taylor's
37
30 Powder Point Avenue
Reuben Drew House
1793
(Annex at 6 Powder Point Avenue)

Of all the residents who took in summer guests in the early 1900s, Sally B. Taylor ran the most popular boarding house. Today, anyone who ever summered in Duxbury during that period remembers "Sally B.'s," as it was affectionately called. Mrs. Taylor's establishment was so well-known that the house at 6 Powder Point Avenue on the triangle with Cove Street, known as the "Annex," was used for overflow guests. Virginia Ludwig and her family often stayed there. She recalled that it was a "tight squeeze, but a great deal of fun." Sally B. came from Philadelphia each summer and brought her help with her. All meals were served at the main house. Between her two houses she could accommodate 25 people, each paying $2.00 per day for meals and lodging. The boarding house was busy in September and October with guests who had to vacate Powder Point Hall when the boys returned for the fall semester.

Eleanor MacDonald often accompanied her mother on visits to Sally B's. She must have been an appealing little girl, for her mother's friends all wanted to kiss her. After this happened numerous times, Eleanor asked her mother to please pin a sign on her dress that read, "Please do not kiss." Eleanor remembers a time when a family of skunks decided Sally B.'s was also a fine place to summer—right under the dining room! The "skunk man" from Abrams Hill was called. When he crawled under the room, Eleanor quickly followed. In the nick of time, someone caught her ankle and dragged her out. If she had succeeded in her adventure, it is certain that constant kissing would have abruptly ceased!

John Smith remembered watching "all those lovely ladies in their long dresses walking around the shore with their little umbrellas, or rocking on the porch while they fanned themselves on a warm summer's day." Sally B.'s commanded a fine view of the Bluefish River and Duxbury Bay, so it is not difficult to understand why the barges were kept busy bringing guests.

Clara Hall Sampson, left, and E.L. Sampson in front of Sally B. Taylor's boarding house in 1904. Below: the house today. (Fran Nichols)

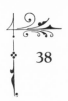

Wadsworth Boarding House

38 72 Washington Street
25 Bayberry Lane
c. 1800

Fred Wadsworth's father, Dr. Edward Perry Wadsworth, owned a number of houses in Duxbury, one of which was directly across Washington Street from St. Margaret's Hospital, now St. Margaret's Convent. After Fred's wife, Abbie, retired from teaching school, they lived here and ran a very successful boarding house during the summer months. Although he was handicapped with a bad leg, Mr. Wadsworth met all of his guests who arrived by train.

Mrs. Wadsworth was a character. Elden Wadsworth, her nephew, recalls going with her to Bachelor and Snyder's Wholesale Beef Company in Boston and watching as she selected the great sides of beef that she deemed would be the tastiest. After completing her business she would take her nephew to the Parker House for luncheon. If there were rolls left over, Aunt Abbie would reach for her capacious black bag and carefully place the remaining rolls in it. Noticing Elden's extreme embarrassment, she gently said to him, "It's all right dear, we paid for them."

Ina Wadsworth helped her mother at the boarding house until she married John Whitechurch, who often summered with them. After her parents died, Ina returned to live in their house. She was a delightful, if eccentric, lady in her later years. According to neighbors, Mrs. Whitechurch had a proclivity for collecting chairs. She often foraged in the town dump, as did many other "pickers." Eventually she had about 200 chairs stored in a barn of an accommodating neighbor.

Wadsworth's Boarding House. The smaller house to the right is the annex. (Virginia Stasinos)

The house today.
(Fran Nichols)

Fred Potter remembered spending a week with his family at the Wadsworth Boarding House. Beth Hutchinson Ryer's family also vacationed there for six summers. This summer retreat was so popular that the house behind it was also used. The two houses were connected by porches where guests enjoyed sitting in their rocking chairs. Eventually, the small house, or annex, was moved a few yards away to its present location on Bayberry Lane. Mr. and Mrs. MacCallum, the present owners, found brass room numbers on each door when they bought the house in 1956.

The main Wadsworth Boarding House is now the home of Mr. and Mrs. Ralph Carver. Before they renovated the kitchen, an early form of refrigeration was still in place. It was a cement cave that measured 6 feet by 8 feet, insulated with sawdust laid a foot thick. Gigantic blocks of ice were passed from the outside through a sturdy door backed with tin.

No record of the Wadsworth Boarding House would be complete without the story of Dr. Edward Perry Wadsworth, who was a successful, if eccentric physician in an era when neither medical degrees nor licenses were required.

Dr. Wadsworth claimed to have healing powers, which Elden says perhaps came from his having traveled extensively with an evangelist. When Mrs. Edwin Noyes' mother was a little girl her mother took her to see Dr. Wadsworth. He went into one of his trances and said that the child had fallen on the third step going downstairs. He had guessed correctly. Dr. Wadsworth did guarantee cures if his patients would eat fresh vegetables from his garden, fresh fish from the sea, and soak up sunshine as they soaked their feet in the salt water. Certainly, to this day this is an unfailing, all-natural prescription for good health in Duxbury!

38 Bay Pond Road
Clarence Smith
1901

39

Above: The south side of the Clarence Smith house as it once looked. (Jennifer Leighton)
Below: The south side of the house today, showing extensive architectural changes. (Fran Nichols)

Clarence Smith, a lobsterman, built his house on a fine piece of land in 1901. His tragic death in his thirties from a ruptured appendix in 1908 left his young widow, Nora, with four children. New income had to be found so she began serving meals to guests. Eventually she took in boarders, as well. Her young daughter, Julia, was a tremendous help.

Nora Smith's first boarder paid $4.00 per week for room and board. Henry Briggs, our second Fire Chief, also stayed with her. During the summer, she was kept busy housing the chauffeurs employed by Powder Point residents. In 1932 Dan and Marie Winsor were her guests when their Winsor House was being renovated.

Mrs. Smith's baking was legendary among the boys at the Powder Point School. Alger Hiss, then a student at the school, regularly purchased doughnuts from Nora. The First National Store on Bluefish River also bought her baked goods which the younger Smith children delivered in their little red wagon.

This house has recently been enlarged and has undergone major renovations.

148 Depot Street
40   Benjamin Prior
1732

From 1871 to 1939 Duxbury was part of the Old Colony Railroad system. There were a roundhouse and a freight house near the depot on the corner of South Station Street across from where the *Duxbury Clipper* building is now.

Henry Fish was a highly respected locomotive engineer. He and his wife lived in a house off Depot Street near the station. After retiring he found time to walk the back trails of Duxbury to locate many of the house sites of Duxbury's earliest settlers. His book *Duxbury Ancient and Modern* and the Fish map, were published in 1924.

Unfortunately, Mr. Fish became severely crippled and it was necessary to augment his pension. In 1915 he and his wife decided to take in boarders. Some of their guests were college boys who had summer jobs as chauffeurs for summer people. Mrs. Fish always called these young men, who were between the ages of 18 and 20, "Mr." which added tremendously to their stature as well as their dignity. Miss Louise Coburn, who summered on South Station Street and who was a close friend of the Fishes, had her chauffeur, John Cassidy, board there. Mrs. Fish was a tiny lady who not only took care of her guests and her husband but raised all of the vegetables served at the table. She regularly had fifteen hungry people to feed at each meal.

The Fishs' guests may have been treated to more than good food and lodging. Isabelle Freeman who lived across the way on Depot Street recalled playing with the Fishs' granddaughter, Helen Alden. One day she was invited to spend the night. The children were

put to bed in the borning room off the winter kitchen with the door left open so they could be heard if necessary. In the middle of the night there was a most unusual noise and an even more unusual sight. The logs which had been piled neatly beside the large hearth in the kitchen began rolling across the room and then just as quickly rolled right back again. This strange occurrence was only one of many.

The George Lyman Richards also owned the house at one time and Mr. Richards remembers being a bit agitated when a window began rattling when everything was absolutely still outside. Why should one window out of five in the room make such a racket?

Those who may be superstitious feel the secret lies with Hitty Tom, the last surviving Indian in Duxbury. Declared a Heathen, she was not allowed to be buried in the cemetery. Sylvanus Prior, who originally owned the Fish property, permitted Hitty Tom to be buried on his land. It is believed her spirit now hovers over the Benjamin Prior house.

Henry Fish and his wife housed railroad men who worked nearby on Depot Street. (Russell Edwards)

620 Washington Street

41 Deacon Loring

1801

Anna and Emily Sears boarded guests at their home in 1916. Their small ad read, "Boarders accommodated during all seasons of the year in one of the most delightfully situated houses in Duxbury, Mass. Nine acres of land bordering on water and the most attractive part of Main Street"[31] (now Washington Street).

Emily Sears had been a highly respected teacher in Duxbury in her younger years. A school report of 1874–75 says, "she is one of our most accomplished and efficient teachers, and the quiet ernest work of the school-room is the best proof of her efficiency and success."[32] Emily received the munificent yearly salary of $612.50. So perhaps summer people helped the Sears sisters to make ends meet.

The Sears' house on Washington Street was in an excellent location for year-round guests, shown in 1920 above and in 1938 at right.   (Russell Edwards)

338 Washington Street
42 Ahira Wadsworth
1803

The house at 338 Washington Street was built in 1803 by Ahira Wadsworth, a prosperous merchant. By 1827, however, the house was lost to creditors, and it was finally bought by Captain Martin Waterman.

Mrs. L.A. Waterman, a granddaughter by marriage of Captain Waterman, took boarders into her home in the 1920s. Mrs. Richmond Arnold recalled Mrs. Waterman as a large and forbidding woman, but Mrs. Allan Waite remembers only the delicious cookies she gave her as she ventured by. Mrs. Waterman also baked cakes which were sold at the Duxbury Handicraft Shop across the street.

This is an elegant house, with flagstones in the cellar and knocker on the front door brought from India by Captain Martin Waterman.

The Ahira Wadsworth house once had numerous boarders. (Above: Mr. and Mrs. William Rice, left: Fran Nichols)

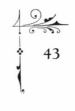

Homewood

43 184 Standish Street
George Bailey
1872

"Come to HOMEWOOD in lovely Duxbury for your summer holiday. A wide piazza with ocean view, an outside dining room, and open land with beautiful sunshine are some of the attractions."[33] The ocean view is now blocked by towering trees, but the house, built in 1872 by George Bailey, stands high on Captain's Hill. Martha Helen Elliott operated this peaceful boarding house which catered to the elderly in the 1930s. Alfresco dining on the back terrace was an added attraction.

The living room of the current owners, Mr. and Mrs. James R.W. Jenner, was previously divided into two guest rooms, and there were two similar guest rooms on the second floor. The Elliots could accommodate approximately 14 people. After Mrs. Elliott's death the house was sold, but Mr. Elliott often came back. He would climb the hillside, pausing to take in the beauty of his surroundings, tears coursing down his cheeks as he recalled a much happier period in his life.

Homewood stood high on Captain's Hill. (Above: Mr. and Mrs. James Jenner, below: Fran Nichols)

464 Washington Street
44 *1885*

500 Washington Street
45 *1900*

In the early 1930s Arthur Murphy rented the Victorian house at 464 Washington Street from Harry Towle and ran it as a boarding house. The house, built in 1885, has 13 rooms with two large living rooms back to back.

Guests ate their meals at Mr. Murphy's Snug Harbor Restaurant across the street. His sister Jessie, who made all the pastries for the restaurant, also took care of the guests at the boarding house.

Mr. and Mrs. Earl Russell and a group of friends would take the whole house for long fall weekends. Amy Sacker moved over to Arthur Murphy's house each year when she was forced to leave the Powder Point Hotel in September because of returning students. She ran the famous Sacker School of Design in Boston.

One of the few Victorian style houses on Washington Street.   (Donald Walker)

This home, built in 1900, was a year-round boarding house run by Mrs. Hansine Nilson in the late 1930s. This must have been a courageous undertaking for her, since both Mrs. Nilson and her daughter were deaf. The meals were served in a dining room with authentic Swedish stenciling on the walls, and on certain days a true Swedish smorgasbord was featured. Dr. Donald Muirhead, who lived next door when he was very young, recalls enjoying this treat. A week's lodging cost between $15.00 and $18.00.

Mr. and Mrs. Rollins Maxwell honeymooned at the Nilsons. Mrs. W. Richmond Arnold's mother, an accomplished actress, was a guest and enjoyed a cigarette now and then, much to the dismay of Mrs. Nilson. Elbert Loth boarded here as a young man, and recalls Mr. Nilson, a carpenter, delighted in telling shady stories at which his wife and daughter always laughed merrily.

Guests enjoyed the Swedish atmosphere at Mrs. Nilson's house.   (Fran Nichols)

Four Winds

46 12 Water Street
Job Sampson
1794

The handsome house at 12 Water Street was built by Job Sampson in 1794. An early bed and breakfast called Four Winds was run by Mr. and Mrs. John Westervelt from 1934 to 1942. The house was opened to guests as stated in a Duncan Hines pamphlet (recommendations for top inns and restaurants):

> Duxbury Mass. 38 Mi. S of Boston A - Guest House: Four Winds, Water St. Open All Year. A Captains old House. 125 years old, now thoroughly restored and modernized. American and European antiques. 8 Guest rms. E. 2 WB $3.50-4.00 Bkfst.

The proximity of the water must have made this a very popular and restful haven for a day or a week.

Job Sampson's house served as a bed and breakfast in the early 1930s   (Fran Nichols).

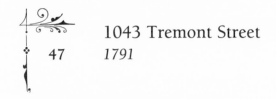

1043 Tremont Street

47 *1791*

This stately house was built in 1791 for Dr. John Allyn, eighth minister of the First Parish Church. In addition to his parish duties he also prepared young boys, some of whom boarded with him, for Harvard. He was a highly respected schoolmaster who seldom dictated to his students how much time should be spent on various subjects, thereby placing considerable responsibility on them. According to the late Herbert E. Walker, Principal of Partridge Academy, Louisa May Alcott was a guest in this house but not during Dr. Allyn's ownership.

Mrs. Martha Hoyt, who owned the house from 1907 until 1942, lived there with her son Frank. They kept chickens, turkeys, and cows. Anna Walker Hardy, who lived across the street with her parents, Mr. and Mrs. Alpheus Walker, recalls that the turkeys would march in military fashion across the road and up the driveway. It was a comical sight.

Miss Lucille Rowe, a favorite cousin, came to help out toward the end of Mrs. Hoyt's life, and she remained as housekeeper for Frank after his mother's death. Miss Rowe eventually inherited the property. To keep busy, she helped with the sale of eggs. One day a customer asked if she would be kind enough to bake her an angel food cake. Miss Rowe's skill at baking soon became widely known, so she opened a bakery in the back ell of the house in the early 1940s.

Desiring companionship, Miss Rowe took in a few year-round boarders, as well as summer visitors. Wedding guests of Mrs. Henry S. Craig stayed there, and Betsy Boyd Stevens met her future husband in this house when Fred's parents, Colonel and Mrs. Frederick Stevens, summered here in 1947 and 1948.

Miss Rowe operated a bakery as well as a
boarding house on Tremont Street.   (Above:
Mr. and Mrs. John M. Dahlen, right: Fran
Nichols)

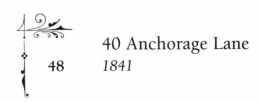

40 Anchorage Lane

48 *1841*

In 1985 Lura Oakes Cushman, who had inherited her house and land from her grandfather, Captain David Cushman, bequeathed the property to the Plymouth County Wildlands Trust. She retained life tenancy. After her death in 1988 the trust took over management of the property along the Bluefish River.

Captain David Cushman commissioned the house to be built while he was at sea. When he returned he was surprised to see that it was taller than he had anticipated. Having been in China and Japan where outdoor living was popular, he decided to add porches, or piazzas as they were called at that time. Lura Cushman's father, Walter, died in 1915. As so often happened, there was a need for money, so her mother began taking in paying guests during the summer. Lura continued the practice after her mother passed away in 1946.

Above: Mary Alden Cushman, Walter Fosdick Cushman and Betty, with Lura's mother, Lucie Hall Cushman on the porch in 1895.   (Above and below: Plymouth County Wildlands Trust)

A talented and interesting lady, Miss Cushman taught at the famed Miss Farmer's School of Cookery for 18 years. She also gave private lessons on chocolate dipping, cooking lobster, and making pastry. Lura kept a daily journal in which there are notations about getting bed chambers cleaned and readied with flowers from her garden and about preparing meals, such as the two she cooked for Eben Ellison when Mrs. Ellison had broken her arm. After Lura told Mr. Ellison about her school (Fannie Farmer's), he sent her home, not only with eggs and meat, but also with a crisp $20 bill.

Upon her retirement in 1960 Lura decided to travel to all the ports her grandfather had been. She went around the world three times, usually by freighter.

Guests at the Cushman house on Anchorage Lane were treated to gourmet meals as they looked out on the captivating view of the Bluefish River. In the house they could enjoy seeing the treasures Lura and her family had collected on their travels.

The house today. (*Fran Nichols*)

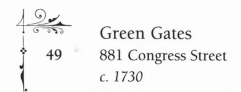

Green Gates

49

881 Congress Street

c. 1730

Located on eight acres of land set back from Congress Street is the home of Mr. and Mrs. Hayden Mason. The house, which was in the Randall family for over two centuries, dates back to the 1730s. At various times it has been a private home, a turkey farm, and an inn. Now barking dogs and meowing cats greet visitors. The Masons raise champion Golden Retrievers and English Cocker Spaniels and run a boarding kennel.

During the 1940s and early 1950s, Mr. and Mrs. Henry M. Griswold ran Green Gates as an inn, "Country and seashore combined." They advertised:

> Our big sixteen room Cape Cod house with the charm of colonial days is untouched by modernization . . . ..Native grown garden products, fresh milk and cheese contribute to our delicious meals served family style. Boston baked beans every Saturday night. Ride over Long Bridge, the longest wooden bridge in Massachusetts to a five mile peninsula of clean sandy beach . . . When you are not swimming or hiking you can play tennis, badminton, croquet, archery or just plain loaf in the sun.

Mrs. William Fletcher of Brookline, Massachusetts spent a few summers here with her parents and sister. Being city children, she and her sister loved the farm which boasted all manner of animals to delight a child. She recalls that the Griswolds were genial hosts who served excellent food and that an aroma of homemade bread permeated the inn.

Although Mrs. Fletcher did not recall anything unusual about Green Gates, the Griswolds themselves were aware of a supernatural presence. In the first years of the Masons' occupancy there was a coldness in the house even on a warm day.

Two strange things occurred even before the Masons had fully moved in. One summer day Mr. Mason had been working on the house. Having to leave before his wife arrived, he left a note saying that if she needed hot water, she should turn on the furnace. Mrs. Mason read the note, and suddenly the furnace came on. She was startled, but erased it from her mind until one night when she and her children were in the house by themselves. After retiring, Mrs. Mason was awakened by a blood-curdling scream emanating from her son's room. She rushed to see what had happened and found him frightened out of his wits. He was so disturbed he threatened to leave the house immediately. Not being able to discover what the problem was, she finally persuaded him to move into another room for the rest of the night. She then went back to bed herself, but could not sleep. Presently a man with arms folded, dressed in black and wearing a tricorner hat, stood staring at her from the foot of her bed. She, too, screamed, but amazingly no one heard her.

The next morning at breakfast she asked her son what had disturbed him so. When he described his nocturnal visitor, even to the tricorner hat, she nodded with complete understanding. They had both been visited by the same apparition.

A year or so later an elderly relative of a former owner returned to Duxbury to see the house again. It was then Mrs. Mason learned of a young man who had fought and been wounded in one of the Indian Wars. He took refuge in this house. The Randalls tried to nurse him back to health. A daughter fell in love with him, but unfortunately he died before they could be married. Perhaps this unfortunate young man returns occasionally in search of his young lady love.

Green Gates combined country and seashore living. (Hayden Mason)

Interestingly, at first the Mason's own dogs were affected. One dog would stand staring in front of the fireplace, his hackles raised, and throw his head back and growl. This same thing occurred with a friend's dog, always in one particular place in the basement.

The Masons' daughter said lights would go on and off by themselves and door latches would go up and down of their own accord. There seemed to be a continuous build up of episodes.

One summer night the Mason's son and some of his friends went swimming in the pool, which had underwater lighting. The friends went home, and he and a house guest, after turning off the pool lights, went back to the house for a bite to eat. Suddenly there was a glow - the pool light had come on. Thinking that there was just a short circuit, they went back to the pool and heard the vent whirring in the pool house, which no one had been near all evening. Going over to turn this off, too, they found the pool house locked from the inside. Undaunted, the intrepid house guest climbed through the window, calmly turned off the vent, and unlocked the door.

Mr. Mason, who had not noticed anything unusual himself, wondered what was happening to his family. Then, one night he, too, had second thoughts. While Mr. Mason was working at his desk in the large loft, the piano at the opposite end of the room began to play. Thinking it was one of their cats pussy-footing on the keys, he yelled and the music stopped, but not for long. Mr. Mason walked across the room and stood transfixed as phantom fingers played across the keyboard!

Thankfully, for the past few years everything has been placid and peaceful at Green Gates. Perhaps the ghosts realize the Masons are friendly, too, and have quietly decided all of them can live together quite happily.

125 Standish Street

50 Sylvanus Sampson
1792

This house was built by Captain Sylvanus Sampson in 1792 and was family-owned until 1983. From 1983 to 1986, Mr. and Mrs. David Stookey, who own the house now, operated a bed and breakfast. Doctors, educators, a curator emeritus from the Currier Gallery in Manchester, New Hampshire, and even a future astronaut stayed here. Soon, because of fires burning cheerfully in the guest bedrooms upon arrival and flowers everywhere, word of mouth kept the house full.

Mrs. Stookey, whose background is English, delighted guests with breakfasts that were half American and half English. The usual fruits, porridge, and eggs were offered, in addition to delicious English fried toast. The American offering was apple pie!

Sylvanus Sampson's 1792 house attracted many guests. (Tony Kelso)

The house today. *(Fran Nichols)*

After the enlightening experience of a visit to Plimoth Plantation, visitors would return with a deeper appreciation of the pureness of this fine old home. It is of Federal architecture and has five fireplaces with another huge one in the cellar. A visit to Captain Sampson's store, which is part of the house, was always saved until guests had been acclimated to the antiquity of their surroundings. Although the store carried mostly necessities, rum probably brought in the most income! It is a tiny museum in itself and looks much as it did 200 years ago.

Guests returned often. A couple from Japan brought little gifts, an astronaut sent the Stookey's son, Benjamin, all kinds of space information; and a thoughtful letter from Texans stated, "Those were the best two days we have ever had." This is surely a home with unique history and character.

51   636 Union Street
Josiah Soule
1708

A part of this very early house dates back to 1708 when it was built by Josiah Soule on a 150-acre farm. The property remained in the Soule family until the Kopkes purchased it in 1953.

In 1983, Mr. and Mrs. Walter Kopke decided to join an organization called the Christian Hospitality Network which offers homes in 50 different areas in the United States. The Kopkes' guests have come from as far away as Australia, Israel, and Japan. Some stay for just a day and others for as long as three weeks. For Walter, the chief chef, blueberry pancakes are a specialty. The Kopkes are friendly, warm hosts who often include a tour of the town as part of their hospitality.

A spirited game of croquet at the Josiah Soule house on Union Street.   *(Walter Kopke)*

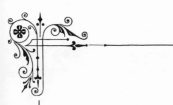

Tearooms

"**I**nnumerable 'Tea-Rooms' dot the New England coast, charming little cottages with surroundings as beautiful as land and sea can make them. They are filled with women eating ices, drinking sugary liquids, cold and delicately colored, or buying the kind of merchandise which is accurately labeled 'Gifts,' and which no purchaser wants to keep, or means to keep, for herself."[34]

Adding to the pleasure of summer guests, Duxbury had its share of these tearooms in the 1920s. Opening a tearoom was a very genteel way for ladies to add to the family's income. Along with tea, there were gifts for sale. Items hand-made over the winter months such as cranberry decorations, rag dolls, and driftwood from the shore were attractively displayed.

Color schemes were emphasized, even including the sandwiches, "jade and ivory were created, using alligator pear and cream cheese."[35] During Prohibition tearooms flourished as they provided healthy nonalcoholic refreshments, especially for ladies.

Ladies carrying parasols would arrive by foot or perhaps by horse and buggy and later by motor. If they used a horse, a "parking" problem developed even at that time. In 1919 Duxbury passed a by-law which read as follows: "No person shall tie or fasten any horse to any ornamental or public shade trees or

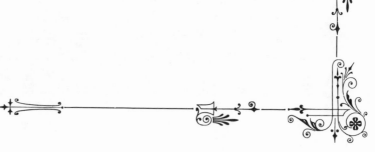

permit a horse to remain unattended and unfastened within six feet of such tree or branches thereof."[36] No matter, the ladies were beautifully attired in bemberg dresses, properly white-gloved with their large picture hats profusely decorated with posies perched upon their heads. Later the skirts shortened and cloche hats became the style but gossiping over the latest fashions with congenial friends and sipping a relaxing cup of tea continued to be enjoyed. This lovely English custom had crossed the ocean.

An afternoon tea party around the turn of the century.

Old Orchard Cottage and Tearoom

52   900 Tremont Street
Early 1700s

The house at 900 Tremont Street, which dates back to the early 1700s, has been restored by Mr. and Mrs. William Trout and Mr. and Mrs. Edward Knecht. An unusual feature of the house is the spring-form dance floor in the ballroom on the second floor. The ballroom had a fireplace which is still framed by hand-painted tiles said to have been designed by an itinerant painter. British soldiers, or "lobsterbacks," as they were disparagingly called, would come from their headquarters in Marshfield to cotillions where a fiddler would play for dancing. The ballroom has now been partitioned to make bedrooms.

Probably a stagecoach stop for travelers between Boston and Plymouth, the house appears deceivingly small, but there is a large ell off the west side.

In 1922, Mr. and Mrs. Christian J. Steele ran a tearoom, the Old Orchard Cottage and Tearoom. In the late 1920s Mr. and Mrs. Thomas Johnson, who rented the house for the summer, continued the restaurant, where they served luncheons and dinners. The Johnsons' two daughters, Mt. Holyoke students at the time, were delighted to help. Homemade cakes and breads as well as ice cream were popular in the restaurant and could be purchased by special order as well.

One summer day when Donald Walker was about ten, his mother asked him to pick some blueberries for supper. Blueberries flourished around the Mayflower Street area where the transfer station is now. Bicycling home, hunger overcame him and he had a sudden thought. Stopping at the Old Orchard Tearoom, he made what he considered a fine deal: one box of

Top: The Old Orchard Cottage and Tearoom was in a pre-Revolutionary house with a spring-form dance floor. (Mr. and Mrs. Edward Knecht) Bottom: The house today. (Fran Nichols)

blueberries for a piece of pie with ice cream. There is no need to mention the greeting he received from his mother when he arrived home.

Locust Tearoom

53   84 Depot Street

c. 1790

On Depot Street northwest of Hall's Corner is an old house with post-and-beam construction and wide floorboards. The walls are plaster made of shells and hair. There is a beehive oven with a crude door made of bog iron.

Long known as the Charles Delano house, it is now owned by Mr. and Mrs. John E. Sheehan. In the 1920s Mr. and Mrs. Harry Nichols owned the property and operated the Locust Tearoom.

Mrs. Nichols was a member of the Community Garden Club of Duxbury and her love of flowers was manifested in her plantings around her house. Mr. and Mrs. Richard Hilliard, later owners, recall the fascinating flowers called "Devils Walking Sticks" which the Nichols had brought from Cape Cod. These plants had tall, spiny stems with lovely large blossoms which created an umbrella effect. The ladies must have admired these flowers before entering for tea. The sign for this tearoom still hangs in the Sheehans' garage.

The Locust Tearoom was on Depot Street, near Hall's Corner.   (Fran Nichols)

1 Bumblebee Lane
54 Peleg Churchill
1794

At the corner of Bumblebee Lane and Washington Street there is a house whose architecture illustrates several different periods in Duxbury's history. Built by Peleg Churchill in 1794, the house has had numerous owners. One was J. deVere Simmons of Boston who lived there from 1903 until 1921. He and his wife served luncheons to some of the children who attended the grammar school that once was located at nearby 354 Washington Street.

In the 1920s Mrs. Buttrick, a summer resident, ran a gift shop and tearoom in the house. She enlarged the kitchen on the east side, making a room with large glass windows and a door opening out onto Washington Street.

Due to remodeling, the well, which was originally located between the house and the barn, is now under the wall between the dining room and the kitchen. Above the second floor there is a turret containing a large water tank. At one time water was pumped from the well up into the tank. From there it would flow by gravity down to the bathrooms and kitchen. This was certainly a unique inside plumbing arrangement.

Several different periods of architecture are revealed in the house at 1 Bumblebee Lane.   (Fran Nichols)

Gay Parasols

55 349 Washington Street

Lot Stetson

1787

The house today.   (Fran Nichols)

Miss Sarah Stetson, who owned the house at 349 Washington Street in the 1920s, rented it to others during the summer months. One of her tenants operated the Gay Parasols tearoom there. The parasols of the name sheltered the ladies as they sipped their tea in the sunny garden; when the weather turned unpleasant, the front parlors offered a delightful atmosphere.

As it has been impossible to find anyone who stopped here for tea, the Gay Parasols must have been a short-lived venture. Only the photo showing its round sign testifies to its existence.

This house is now part of the historic district. It was built by Lot Stetson in 1787, and since then, the only architectural change has been the addition of a small dormer on the north side.

Below: Ladies enjoying their tea under the umbrellas at Gay Parasols.   (Margery L. MacMillan)

Mrs. Shaw's Tearoom
56 273 Harrison Street

Mrs. Josephine Hartwell Shaw, a large, buxom woman, ran an excellent tearoom here in the 1920s. The house, called Three Acres, overlooked a pond on which a pair of graceful swans glided back and forth. Guests were served on one of two screened porches or on a charming terrace across the lawn. In inclement weather they enjoyed tea before a cavernous fireplace inside.

Homemade biscuits, cinnamon toast, tea, and cakes were the usual fare, but Mrs. Shaw also served luncheons and dinners by reservation. For both meals tinted finger bowls shaped like large flower blossoms added a pretty and colorful touch to the table settings. For lunch a lobster roll cost $1.50. Irene Walker recalled being a waitress and helping in the kitchen. She and Ruth Krueger put in "long, long hours" for which they were paid "very, very little." Ruth remembers spending afternoons standing on a stool washing dishes, then turning to the job of cracking open all the lobsters, and finally grinding beans for homemade coffee.

The young waitresses giggled over one customer whom they nicknamed "cracked ice." As soon as she appeared in the tearoom, she would demand a pitcher of ice, the contents of which she apparently enjoyed chewing.

The tearoom thrived as the ever-vigilant Mrs. Shaw inspected everything before it left the kitchen. She was

Mrs. Shaw's Tearoom as shown on a post card and the house today. (Above: Fran Nichols)

Left: Detail of necklace in gold, jade, and glass made by Josephine Hartwell Shaw, c. 1915. (Museum of Fine Arts, Boston, gift of Mrs. Atherton Loring) Above: The antique shop.

also frugal. Once, after the waitresses had watched a particular piece of chocolate cake with green icing go out to three or four different tables, always coming back untouched, they decided to divide it between them. Of course at that very moment Mrs. Shaw appeared and the waitresses were properly chastised! The girls were supposed to pool their tips, but sometimes stray nickels and dimes would find their way home inside their shoes.

An added attraction to the tearoom was the well-stocked antique shop called The Duxbury Shop in a nearby building run by Mrs. Shaw's friend, Elizabeth Morris Leete. Eunice Estes Dohoney, who worked at the tearoom when she was 14, has some Rose Medallion china Mrs. Shaw purchased at the shop as a wedding present for her.

The capable Mrs. Josephine Shaw was also artistic. During the winter months, she designed and made jewelry which was displayed at the Boston Arts and Crafts Shop. Mrs. Shaw's pieces were so expensive that one local customer declared, "I might as well have gone to Tiffany's!"

Mrs. Shaw also cared a great deal about Duxbury's welfare. She served in an advisory capacity on an early planning board with Percy Walker.

In 1932 Mrs. Shaw moved her business to 567 Bay Road. Mrs. Chester Sampson helped there after her restaurant, The Bridge Food Shoppe, closed. Mrs. Sampson's shredded wheat biscuits became a specialty. The ladies particularly enjoyed the mushroom sandwiches which Mrs. Kenneth Bunten recalls as being delicious. However, the tearoom at the Bay Road location was never quite the same as the original.

Tidewater Teatable

57   644 Washington Street

1920s

The house at 644 Washington Street is on part of the site where Zenas Faunce, an anchor-smith, had his small foundry in the mid-1800s. There he forged ironware which was used on Duxbury ships. The bog iron ore was collected from the many bogs in town. The Washington Street house of Zenas Faunce's son, Zenas, Jr., has fine grill work which probably came from his father's foundry.

The little house by the Bluefish River bridge, which has always been known as Tidegates, was once a tearoom called the Tidewater Teatable. Zenas Faunce's granddaughter, Isadore Hill, and her mother operated the tearoom in the 1920s. Its unique, panoramic view of the Bluefish River and mill pond obviously lured guests to enter and relax.

Later, Isadore and her sister, Versey Hill, decided to open a gift shop and bakery across the street at 1 Fort Hill Lane in the house known as the Bo's'ns Locker. This little building, which has served in so many different capacities, was also part of their grandfather's estate.

The house which was once Tidewater Teatable looks much the same today as it did in the post card below, sent in 1911. (Left: Robert Dente, right: Fran Nichols)

Duxbury, Mass. Blue River Bridge

The Copper Kettle

58 290 High Street

1758

In 1922 Miss Nellie Mahoney, like so many others during this period, thought a tearoom and gift shop would be an interesting and profitable venture. She hung a copper kettle outside the front door of her house and opened for business.

Miss Mahoney, a pretty lady with lovely blue eyes and gray hair, always dressed in the latest fashions. A charming hostess but a city girl at heart, she found wrestling with a large wood stove and drawing water with a hand pump too much, so she remained in business only a short time. Instead, Nellie Mahoney found an occupation much more to her liking: in 1924 she married John E. Hobill.

The house is thought to have been built by James Barstow in 1758. It boasts a large middle room with gunstock posts and a huge fireplace with a beehive oven.

The Copper Kettle was in this charming eighteenth-century cape house.   (Above: Andrew Pollock, below: Fran Nichols)

Sweetheart Tearoom

59   380 Tremont Street
1900

This small eating establishment was run by Mr. and Mrs. Arthur L. Parker from 1924 until 1927. Mrs. Eileen Parker Young, their daughter, remembers that the name was chosen after her family had seen a similar place on a trip along the Mohawk Trail. Mrs. Parker, a fine cook as well as an amiable lady, was nicknamed "Mollie Sweetheart."

The popular speciality at the Sweetheart Tearoom was waffles offered at "All you can eat for 50 cents." Guests from Tinkertown Acres on Island Creek Pond crowded the place on weekends.

The Sweetheart Tearoom was famous for its waffles.   (Fran Nichols)

Bambolina Tearoom

60   782 Temple Street
c. 1700

This popular, though somewhat isolated, tearoom was located in an old house north of the village. The house faced Old Cordwood Path, which was laid out in 1742.

Owned by Clarence and Adeline Lippincott, the tearoom was really a restaurant specializing in Italian cooking. (Bambolina means "little doll" in Italian.) According to Tony Amado who cared for the grounds at the tearoom, Mr. Lippincott worked in the Fall River Shipyard, so it was left to Mrs. Lippincott to run the establishment, with the help of their daughters.

Mrs. Lippincott met her husband in St. Petersburg, Russia, far from her native Volterra, Italy, where her family owned many vineyards. Her education in the use of good wines added considerably to the kitchen aromas at the Bambolina. This Duxbury restaurant remained in business from 1925 until just before World War II.

The Bambolina Tearoom on Temple Street specialized in Italian food.   (Russell Edwards)

Blackberry Acres Tearoom
61 212 High Street
c. 1835

Miss Clara E. Lewis, who taught art in the East Providence, Rhode Island schools for 64 years, ran Blackberry Acres Tearoom during the summer months in the 1930s. Miss Lewis' artistic talent was evident in her attractive tearoom. She also turned her talents to community affairs, for whenever a poster or sign was needed for a bazaar or church supper, she always obliged. She never forgot a birthday, and her distinctive, handmade cards were much appreciated, in spite of her unorthodox method of delivering them. Miss Lewis owned a few cows. Rounding up her favorite, she would hang the card around the cow's neck, point "old bossy" in the direction of the birthday celebrant, and give her a whack on the rump. As Miss Lewis was always thanked, her dispatcher proved not only inexpensive but reliable as well.

This house was built in the 1800s by Miss Lewis' grandfather, Joseph Lewis, who also helped build the West Duxbury Methodist Church in 1868.

Below: The Blackberry Acres Tearoom was on historic High Street. (Philip Swanson) Right: The house as it looks today. (Fran Nichols)

Ann's Kitchen
62 280 Tremont Street

This small tearoom in the Island Creek area had a fine view of the Mill Pond just as the house does today. The tearoom was run by two sisters, Ann and Winifred McLeod. They had worked at the Waltham Watch Factory in the 1920s but decided to open the tearoom in the early 1930s.

The house was built on a hillside so the first floor was high over the pond. Here tea was served. There was also a screened porch where customers would sit during the summer. In the winter the guests could watch men cutting ice and filling Cushing's ice house at the pond's edge.

The McLeod sisters apparently enjoyed this venture, but towards the end of the 1930s they changed their venue, reopening their tearoom in Waltham.

Ann's Kitchen was located in this house overlooking the Mill Pond at Island Creek.   (Fran Nichols)

Log Cabin Tearoom
63 Alden Street
Charles L. Alden
1920s

The Log Cabin Tearoom was built in the 1920s by Charles L. Alden, a direct descendent of John Alden and brother of Arthur Alden who later managed White Brothers Dairy Bar on Bay Road. The building, located directly behind the John Alden house, was originally built to accommodate tourists visiting the famous landmark. The meals and tea were so tasty, however, that word-of-mouth advertising made the little restaurant very popular. There was a gift shop in the front of the building where bags of home-roasted peanuts were offered as a specialty.

Doris Baker and Bessie Soule worked at the Log Cabin when they were very young. The girls had to dress as Pilgrims. Being given only one costume, they raced against time to have it washed, starched, and ironed each day before going to work.

A guest was enjoying her tea one afternoon when Bessie, much to her amusement, overheard her say, "I simply cannot understand why John Alden would build his fine home so close to the railroad!"

The Log Cabin Tearoom today. (Fran Nichols)

Singing Clams

An amusing article was reprinted from the *New York Times* in the *Boston Transcript* of July 31, 1915. It is titled: DUXBURY'S SINGING CLAMS.

From Duxbury, Mass. comes the news that the singing clams, for which that resort has long been famous, are now facing extermination and soon will be relegated to the past along with the dodo, side hill gouger and plesiosaurus. Phineas Railnettor, choirmaster of the little church on the hill in Duxbury . . . was in New York yesterday. "The singing clams have been one of Duxbury's greatest attractions since the landing of the Pilgrims," he said, "and the rapacity and inordinate appetites of the newcomers of the summer colony are responsible for the fact that they are rapidly being wiped out. By newcomers I mean those of the summer colony who have been coming to Duxbury for only the past fifty years. The others, the genealogical aristocrats of the colony, have been coming to Duxbury since before the discovery of the sacred cod–and that, of course, was long before the Revolution."

The article goes on to say that, . . . rather than myth, these clams are to be found along the shore and mud flats and they are quite different from any other clam in the world because of their aversion to water! When the tide comes in they burrow down into the soft bottom for a few inches and wait until the water recedes. Then they zig-zag through the ooze, lie outside their holes, open their shells and sing! The natives and fishermen of Duxbury never ate the clams. In fact, they were known to feed them cranberries and the children called them 'The Little Angels of the Bay.' Now all of this is changed. A crude business person discovered that each voice came from a clam that was perfectly good to eat and before long their fame as steamed clams spelled the beginning of the end. Now clam forks are part of everyone's baggage when they move to Duxbury each summer . . .

Detail of "Clam Digger in Duxbury" by John Joseph Enneking. (Mr. and Mrs. Abbot W. Vose)

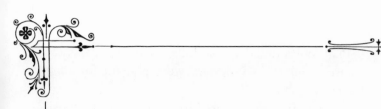

Restaurants

t Duxbury's earliest eating establishments, the seventeenth-century ordinaries, men ate together around a central tavern table. At later boarding houses, patrons usually ate family style around a large table hosted by the boarding house owner. During the nineteenth-century heyday of hotels and inns, guests were on the American Plan (all meals included) so they naturally ate in the hotel dining rooms.

The custom of eating at home continued in twentieth-century Duxbury. Some of the earlier tearooms expanded into full-fledged successful restaurants, but in general the town is not known for its "eating out" population.

In spite of Duxbury's recent growth, the larger restaurants depend on out-of-towners, while the smaller ones usually have enjoyed dependable local patronage. The proximity of Route 3 plus Duxbury's historic attractions continue to entice visitors from afar. Guests often arrive planning to spend at least a half day. By midday, or toward evening, they begin to fill our restaurants where, often in historic settings, they enjoy a most welcome, relaxing meal.

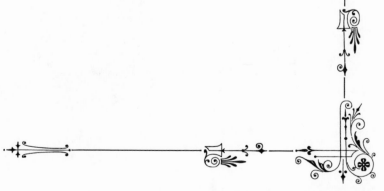

The Milepost

Bailey's Corner

"Let's eat at the Milepost!" This refrain has echoed around Bailey's Corner for many years, although the ownership and the name of the restaurant have changed several times.

It all began in the early 1920s with a rustic roadside stand that had two screened porches with canvas drops for protection against a nor'easter. Mr. and Mrs. Eugene Page operated Page's Stand on the property rented from Mr. John C. Runkle. Mrs. Page was a shy person, but capable and thoughtful. Once, she decided that one of the waitresses needed a new dress, so, after long hours at the restaurant, she stitched up a flowered one which Emily Loring, the recipient, prized. Emily and Nancy Glass, who worked for Mrs. Page as teenagers, recall that a complete dinner cost about 50 cents. Their weekly wage was $8.00. The tips were small, but a dollar was a dollar, hard work was the norm, and the youngsters were grateful for their summer jobs.

When the Pages retired from the restaurant business in 1929, Mildred A. ("Ma") Pierce moved her small business to this site, leasing it for the first few years and acquiring it in the middle 1930s. Previously, in 1926, she had purchased a tiny shop next to Sweetser's Store from David Goodspeed. At the time Ma was raising six children with no help from anyone. The fragrant aroma of frying doughnut holes was too enticing for most to pass up, so her small business was an immediate success. She was asked to supply the Duxbury Yacht Club with doughnuts for many of their parties.

The ever-hungry young crowd appreciated Ma Pierce's talents and followed her to the Bailey's Corner location. They liked her and she liked them, often lending them $5.00 or $10 . . . at a time. No one ever failed to pay her back. Ma Pierce was a courageous,

A photo from the restaurant's earliest days. (Nina Burns)

The Milepost as it looks today. (Fran Nichols)

generous, and remarkable woman. She gave of herself and what little she had, especially during the Depression years when she never turned anyone away.

From 1929 until she retired in 1947, Ma Pierce prepared and cooked everything served at the restaurant. Her fried clams were legendary, as was her lemon sponge pie. Many customers tried in vain to purchase her sponge pie recipe. Her daughter, Mrs. Nina M. Burns, never saw her use a cookbook—she didn't even own one!

Ma was probably the originator of the drive-in theater locally. A cigarette company gave her a screen for advertising purposes, which was set up in the grove where the parking lot is now. Movies were shown to the patrons as they were enjoying clam chowder at the picnic tables.

One day a midwestern couple, dressed in hiking and climbing outfits, arrived from Plymouth for lunch at Ma Pierce's. They had been bitterly disappointed with their visit, for they had come prepared to scale Plymouth Rock!

Later, a Plymouth realtor purchased the property and the restaurant continued in business under Knute Luttropp who named it The Corner Cupboard. Eventually, Margaret and Doris Viall, along with Thelma Snow of Marshfield, rented the property from him. Their menus were more elaborate and the food continued to be delicious.

In 1956, the Carl Schaffer family bought the restaurant and made many changes. First, they had Walter Prince move the building back from the street onto a new foundation. Francis Swift supervised the extensive renovations, among them making up the fireplace with its fieldstones and wooden mantel from a Catholic rectory in Pembroke.

The Schaffers named the restaurant The Milepost because the site was a mile from Tinkertown, South Duxbury, and Island Creek. The Milepost was a family undertaking. Mr. and Mrs. Carl Schaffer, their sons and daughters-in-law, and all the grandchildren participated. Only freshly grown food was used and all of the baking was done on the premises. According to Dick Schaffer, the heart and soul of the enterprise was his mother Greta, who was a superior cook. One of her specialties was pecan pie. Ruth Wakefield also recalled having enjoyed "the best stuffed lobster she had eaten anywhere" at The Milepost. At this time the restaurant did not have a bar, although liquor was served from the kitchen.

One evening at about six o'clock Bill Ellison appeared at the door in his work clothes and looking a bit muddy. He handed Dick Schaffer a brown paper bag and said he would like its contents for supper. Slightly taken aback, Dick asked him what was in the bag. Bill replied, "Asparagus, just picked it in my garden and I'd like a nice steak to go with it." This was accomplished but at the end of his meal when Bill asked how much he owed, there was a pause. Finally Dick replied, "Damned if I know!"

In 1964 the Schaffers sold the property to Robert and Ruby Simpson who kept the name Milepost for a while, but later changed it to The Dory. The Simpsons added a full cellar to the building. They also added a bar and stayed open until 1 a.m. The popular specialties now were sirloin steak and seafood, with the cost of a complete dinner climbing to $4.95.

After a few years, Mr. and Mrs. Simpson sublet the restaurant to Paul and Bob Lundbaum who called it The Brothers II. Their ownership was short-lived. In 1979 Dr. and Mrs. George Henderson purchased the restaurant, renaming it The Milepost. The Hendersons raised the ceilings and changed some doors, so that the dining room was opened up considerably without being enlarged. Mrs. Henderson's eye for interior decorating added much to make this popular eating place very attractive. Like the Schaffers, the Hendersons made managing and running the restaurant a family affair.

In 1982 the Hendersons sold The Milepost to Mr. and Mrs. John Johnson. Owning a restaurant was a new adventure for them, but Mr. Johnson holds a degree in economics and his business acumen has helped considerably.

In April 1984, the Boston Herald's article "Stepping Back in Time in Duxbury," suggested that after visiting Duxbury's historic sites, travelers should conclude their day with a meal at The Milepost. Local Duxburyites have also continued to appreciate this family-style restaurant which began its life as Page's Stand at Bailey's Corner over 60 years ago.

Milepost Pecan Pie

3 eggs
1 cup light brown sugar
1 tablespoon butter
1 cup light Karo corn syrup
1 cup pecan halves
1 teaspoon vanilla
1/2 teaspoon salt

Cream butter and sugar together. Add syrup, well-beaten eggs, salt, and vanilla. Add pecans. Turn mixture into unbaked pie crust. Bake at 400° for 40 minutes.

(Jetta Schaffer)

The Bridge Food Shoppe

65   661 Washington Street

The original part of this structure at the water's edge by the Bluefish River Bridge was used in a shipbuilding yard. Later Harrison Stranger had a plumbing business here. After Loren Nass bought the property he leased it to Mr. and Mrs. Chester Sampson. In 1931 Mrs. Sampson opened The Bridge Food Shoppe.

Gertrude Sampson was a large, jolly lady. Her little restaurant quickly thrived, so more room was needed. Her husband, a builder-contractor, not only built living quarters for his family but also added a cheerful dining room with many windows on the south side. The long and narrow kitchen was like a galley but had a lovely view overlooking the water. The dining room held about 40 people at tables made by Mr. Sampson.

Each table was a different color, with matching glasses, creamers, and sugar bowls, so the restaurant had the essence of a lovely, seashore flower garden. Chauffeurs from Powder Point ate there regularly, paying $8–10 a week for three meals a day. John Alden, a descendent of the original John, sold ice cream cones on the north side of the building.

Mrs. Sampson's daughter, Marjorie Phillips, assisted her mother in the kitchen. Another daughter, Dorothy Doyle, and her friend Marjorie Loring, who came from Miss Farmer's School of Cookery in Boston, were waitresses. Mrs. Loring recalls that the children swimming in Bluefish River often put on quite a show for the diners.

Mrs. Sampson was astute and understanding with her help. Her employees were told they might eat anything from the menu, even lobster. After having cracked open so many of the shellfish for the custom-

Below: Young waitresses, Dorothy Doyle and Marjorie Loring take a breather from their duties. (Marjorie Phillips)   Right: Mrs. Sampson.

View of the south side of the house that was once the Bridge Food Shoppe. (Fran Nichols)

ers, her help were soon perfectly content with the simpler fare.

After her marriage, Dorothy Doyle lived in the Drew House, the home of the Duxbury Rural and Historical Society. She and her husband had a dog named Bubsie who often was sent to The Bridge Food Shoppe on an errand with a basket in his mouth. Mrs. Sampson would load him up, and he would return safely, very pleased with his delivery. Next to the Drew house was the First National Store, and men often congregated there to exchange news and views. They would watch Bubsie with amusement, and at-

tempt to lure him from his appointed route. But this remarkable dog was not to be diverted, and soon learned to give the First National a wide berth, much to the delight of the onlookers.

The Bridge Food Shoppe was in business just under ten years. Soon after it closed, Mrs. Sampson invited the Alliance of the Unitarian Church to hold a fundraising bridge party at the restaurant. She supplied all of the refreshments, including a special treat or two. Gertrude Sampson, known also as the "Apple Pie Lady," did an outstanding job serving the Duxbury community.

The Winsor House

66   390 Washington Street
John Howland
1809

John Howland built the house known as the Winsor House in 1809 on land deeded to him by his father-in-law, Nathaniel Winsor. In 1842 the Howlands sold their home to sea captain Daniel Loring Winsor for $750. The captain's son George later inherited it. George and his wife Harriet were said to live rather formally for Duxbury. She was very homesick for her native England. After their first two children were born Mrs. Winsor persuaded her husband to move to Kent, England, where they raised their family of six. George did not wish to sell his fine home in Duxbury, however, so he closed it up. It remained uninhabited for over 30 years, looking lonely and forlorn. Marian Huckins wrote, "The grass had grown long . . . the gates were forbiddingly shut . . . the blinds closed, it

stood silently waiting through the years." Children called it a ghost house. Later Daniel Winsor, George and Harriet Winsor's son, returned to this country. He served as a bo'sun in the first World War. Later, while working for a construction company, he met his second wife, Marie. Together they went to Florida where Dan worked at the Allison Hotel in Miami Beach. After George and Harriet Winsor died, the heirs decided that Dan should have the house in Duxbury.

In 1932 passersby on Washington Street were startled to see activity at number 390. Shutters came off and the house was spruced up. Daniel and Marie Winsor had returned not only to take up residence, but to open an inn! With little money, but plenty of talent, they went to work. Dan modernized the plumbing and heating. When the Pilgrim Church was remodeled, wonderful old pine boards were found in the basement which were used to make tavern tables, benches, and a fine bar still in use in the pub today.

An early post card of the Winsor House showing the carriage house as a separate building.

There was a wassail bowl at the Winsor House every Sunday during the winter months and mugs with owners names hung over the bar. The carriage house was decorated with halters. A Lucky Strike vending machine advertised cigarettes for 10 cents a package. With Dan as the genial bartender and Marie the hostess who combined southern charm with sound business sense, they were ideal innkeepers.

The Earl Russells and their friends often enjoyed lunch at the Winsor House before playing golf. "We'll be back," were their parting words as they left for the links. Dan Winsor heard it so many times he finally named a cocktail "We'll be back."

Dan and Marie Winsor behind the bar at the Winsor House. (Charles M. Werly)

It was a sad day when the Winsors decided to retire after 20 years of gracious hospitality. George Crowell and Mrs. Edwin Noyes joined the couple for a final champagne toast, after which they threw their glasses into the fireplace. The 169-year chain of Winsor ownership was about to be broken.

Winsor House next became Chez Lucien. Mr. Lucien Vivas, who had been a steward for the French steamship lines, owned a restaurant on Massachusetts Avenue in Boston. He was forced to leave when the Massachusetts Turnpike was constructed and decided to move to the country. Although he was a superior chef and a hard worker, Mr. Vivas never felt Duxbury accepted his French cuisine. He and his wife became discouraged and then sold out and moved to Florida.

David Wells, who also owned Fiddler's Green, purchased the property in 1969, once again calling it The Winsor House. Unfortunately, as he said, "Running two restaurants in a non-eating-out town, plus attempting a continental menu, did not work out financially." However, it was during Mr. Wells' ownership that the carriage house, which is attached to the main building, was renovated and put into use.

In 1971 the Connor brothers, David and Richard, became owners, with brother Kevin joining them a year later. They decided to bring back the country atmosphere to the restaurant.. With a simplified menu prepared by Rick, Kevin tending bar, and David acting as innkeeper, the establishment was a success.

Living in a small town has many advantages when people take time to be friendly. Although David had been reminded to renew his liquor license due the first of the year, he and his brothers were so busy getting ready for their initial New Year's Eve party that they forgot to do it. At the height of the festivities Paul Barber, a selectman at that time, walked in and asked how things were going. "Just fine, Paul," said David. "Everyone seems happy. You're just in time for a toast.

One minute before midnight." "Haven't you forgotten something David?" asked Paul. Then, looking at David's blank expression, Paul reached into his breast pocket and, without a word, handed him his liquor license. The New Year could now legally begin!

The Connor brothers gave Marie Winsor a reception on one of her infrequent trips back to Duxbury. She greatly appreciated it, although it must have brought back many nostalgic memories. Her husband Dan had died a few years earlier.

In 1976 the last thing David O'Connell ever expected to do, although he was an excellent cook, was to run a restaurant, much less an inn. A friend who knew the Winsor House was for sale persuaded him to consider this possibility. He reluctantly agreed. Once here, David could not resist the charm of the house. In two days the transaction had been completed.

The O'Connells made restoring this historic building, the carriage house with its outdoor patio, and the charming English garden their priorities. They also renovated rooms upstairs for overnight guests.

On June 5, 1989, after twelve years of innkeeping, Mr. and Mrs. O'Connell turned over the reins to three enthusiastic couples, the Maguires, the Driscolls, and the Sanborns. Myles Maguire and Bob Driscoll had experience with Marriott; Scott Sanborn is a silent partner. The three husbands and wives have specific jobs but they are flexible and versatile. When something needs doing everyone pitches in. Bob Driscoll is the all-important king of the kitchen. The Winsor House Inn is now open seven days a week and will continue as an inn with accommodations for eight people.

It is reassuring to see cheerful candlelight twinkling from the windows of the inn, especially on a cold winter's night, and to know that John Howland's house continues to be looked after with appreciation of its place in Duxbury's history.

Mary Hackett's • Sun Tavern

67 500 Congress Street
1741

The front part of this farmhouse was built in 1741. At the end of the nineteenth century it was owned by Lysander Walker, who gained dubious fame when his story was published in the October 21, 1928 issue of the *Boston Herald* in an article titled "Last Duxbury Hermit."

> After the death of his wife, Lysander removed himself from the outside world preferring to live with his memories of bygone days. Friends and neighbors did what they could for him, supplying vegetables from their gardens and milk from their cows. He always flew the American flag outside his door each morning and if anything was needed, he hung a white cloth out of a corner window. His neighbors worried about him but that is the way it was until one morning Gladys Belknap Huff's sister, then aged 11 and on her way to school, noticed that flag had been hung upside down. She thought this was odd so decided to go in and tell her old friend he had made a mistake. At first she thought he was asleep but then, horrified, she noticed the smoking revolver still clutched in his hand. Lysander had signalled one last time in a way which would never be quite forgotten.

After Walker's death Father Francis Keagan purchased the property for his summer residence. He befriended Mary Hackett and financed her education at Salem State Normal School. In the early 1930s he suggested she take over his house and run it as a restaurant. There were cottages too, and in one of these Mary had a gift shop.

This small eating place was successful. It was "situated in the heart of the cranberry plantations and was famous for its quaintness, beautiful flowers and delightful meals." [37] During the winter months Mary

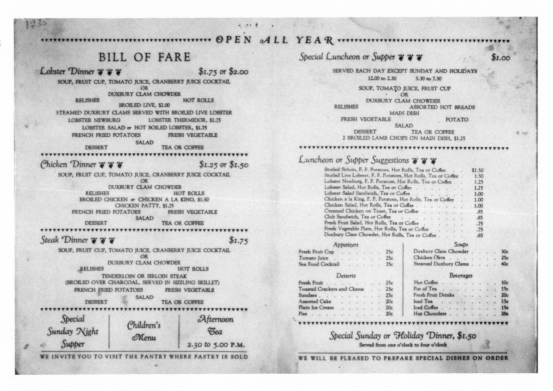

Hackett operated the Alibi Restaurant on Worth Avenue in Palm Beach.

During World War II Mary Hackett was hired by Howard Johnson to run the concession for Necco Sweets at the Watertown Arsenal. After the war, she reopened her Duxbury restaurant, but only for a year. From then until 1964 there were numerous owners, all keeping the name Mary Hackett's.

David Wells bought Mary Hackett's in 1964 for $40,000. He changed the name to Fiddler's Green Restaurant to convey the feeling of an English pub. An admirer said, "David's great food, energy, and personality put this spot on the map." David also put the house on the map, for he claimed it was inhabited by a ghost, and one who had a few tricks up his sleeve at

that! Each night when the restaurant was being closed down and every candle extinguished on the tables, just one would be relit as David, the last to leave, was about to walk out the door. Early one morning, when he was alone opening boxes of supplies in the cellar, carton after carton came tumbling down the stairs on top of him. Of course David was teased about his infamous ghost whom he named Lysander. Late one night the alarm went off and the police arrived to investigate. After checking the entire building and finding nothing, they closed the door and started up the path. Suddenly, each officer heard footsteps in the restaurant. With guns drawn, they entered the house but found no one! Never again was David ridiculed about his ghost.

In March 1973 the Chart House took over the Fiddler's Green Restaurant. The managers of this well-known chain of restaurants invested a considerable amount of money in refurbishing the building and updating the decor. As the Chart House, the restaurant featured a steakhouse menu.

Lance Mann purchased the assets from the Chart House in 1983 and changed the name to Buck's Tavern. Although this was a short-lived venture for him, the antiquity of the house and its atmosphere were not lost on Mr. Mann or his staff. He wrote, "People have left to the place part of themselves, their hearts and their souls. Couples have promised to be true to each other for life here; those whose worldly concerns no longer exist have been toasted here. The old building exudes a certain friendliness which has left its mark on a number of people."

In March of 1986, Mr. and Mrs. William Ekasala reopened the restaurant as the Goose Summer. This unusual name came from the word *gossamer*, which has a French derivation, *gos* and *somer*, referring to a mild period of weather in November when geese are eaten. Mr. Ekasala wrote a delightful poem to this effect which appeared on his menu. The Goose Summer was primarily a family operation. Daughter Terry tended bar and was responsible for the art which decorated the rooms. Her sister Danielle was cashier.

The ghost paid the new owners a visit by opening and closing doors. They were delighted, although confused, because at Hell's Blazes, their former restaurant in Middleborough, a friendly spirit had haunted them. They wondered if it had followed them to Duxbury.

Frederick Dearing, who had first been chef for the Ekasalas at Hell's Blazes and later its owner, bought the Goose Summer on January 1, 1987, renaming it Sun Tavern. He must have had a soothing effect on the place, for no ghosts appeared. Finding it difficult to run two important restaurants simultaneously, in July 1989, Mr. Dearing sold Sun Tavern to Nancy Mathey, proprietor of Caitlin Catering Service. Along with managing the restaurant, Mrs. Mathey continues her catering but it is now handled from the tavern. The name Sun Tavern has been retained.

This house has stood along Congress Street since 1741. (Top: Fran Nichols, bottom: Robert Dente)

68 Snug Harbor Restaurant
447 Washington Street
c. 1930

Above: An advertisement from 1945. Below: The old blacksmith shop before it became a tearoom and restaurant. (Robert Dente)

Some Duxbury residents remember when the building housing the Talbot's store was a blacksmith's shop. At the turn of the century when the blacksmith closed, the building was transformed into the Blacksmith Shop Tearoom. Later it became the Snug Harbor Restaurant, owned and operated by Arthur Murphy, who had run a small cellar restaurant in New York City. Mr. Murphy built a long addition to the rear of the building so diners could enjoy a lovely water view.

Through the 1930s and 1940s Arthur Murphy served choice New England dishes to natives and visitors alike. He became famous for his fine soups, crabmeat souffle, and shore dinners, which were prepared with the help of his sister, Jessie Murphy Mac-Cormack, and Greta Schaffer.

During World War II Arthur Murphy fed the troops stationed in Duxbury to guard the Cable House.

These men bivouacked directly across the street in Sprague Hall. Mrs. MacCormack recalls that the soldiers often would help both in the kitchen and waiting on table. During this time the restaurant was almost demolished, but not by the enemy. One evening there was some difficulty lighting the stove and one of the soldiers offered to help. Thinking it was kerosene, he added gasoline to the fuel line. The chimney blew right off the building and the rest of the company retreated in every direction!

Mr. Murphy enjoyed acting and was one of the leaders of the Duxbury Players. Many of his theater friends came to Duxbury, including, it is said, Hollywood star Ramon Navarro. Probably few residents recall this screen idol who made so many feminine hearts flutter in the 1920s.

James Westaway McCue wrote in *Cape Cod Holiday*, "Snug Harbor (Restaurant) is a spot that the visitor to historic Duxbury will long remember."[38]

The building today. (Fran Nichols)

White Brothers Dairy Bar

69   10 Bay Road
1930s

The White Brothers Milk Company opened a dairy bar at the head of Bay Road in the 1930s. Arthur Alden was the cheerful, outgoing manager who worked 12 to 14 hours a day behind the counter. Arthur Alden was ninth in line from John I, and in 1941 *Life* Magazine carried an article about him. However he was a modest man and not overly impressed with his ancestry. He was also the caretaker at the John Alden House, where his wife responded to a honk of the horn when a tourist wished to tour this famous Duxbury landmark.

This restaurant on Bay Road changed hands often. At one time three generations of the Chester Sampson family worked there: Mrs. Sampson; her daughter, Mrs. Marjorie Phillips; and her granddaughter, Mrs. Richard Lippard. It was once a Howard Johnsons, then Myles Standish Restaurant, and just before demolition, the Duxbridge. In 1983 the building was purchased and razed by Attorney James Pye, Jr. and two partners. An office complex very similar in style was erected on the site.

*Arthur Alden.
(Alfred Eisenstaedt,
Life Magazine
© Time Warner,
Inc.)*

The Chowder Bowl • The Swedish Sandwich Shop
70 446 Summer Street
c. 1843

The origins of this house have been traced back to 1843, but it was probably built much earlier. The barn, with its solid oak flooring, was used for good old-fashioned neighborhood dances and became known as the "Dancing Barn." At these hoedowns or "kitchen sprees,"[39] local swains tried to impress their lady loves with some fancy steps. One young Lockinvar who had been attentive to a daughter of the neighborhood found himself outdistanced by a rival. He sorrowfully remarked to the fair damsel, "Well, Saphroney, I guess yer peppermint days are over."[40]

In 1936 J. Percival Sears purchased the property. He and his wife, Janet, opened The Chowder Bowl, adding the ell in the rear which served as the dining area for guests. Mr. Sears worked in Boston in the insurance business so The Chowder Bowl, primarily open on weekends, was more of a hobby than a business. Lobster salad and clam chowder were extremely popular specialties.

In 1946 Mr. and Mrs. Walter Anderson became the owners and changed the name to The Swedish Sandwich Shop because of their knowledge of Scandinavian cooking. Later, they decided to give up the restaurant and take in overnight guests. They converted the dining room into two bedrooms and the loft in the "Dancing Barn" became three more.

Today Mr. and Mrs. Richard Harris enjoy this antique cape as their private home. Mrs. Harris cooks on the huge iron range on which delicacies still bubble cheerfully for invited guests just as they did 40 years ago.

Two restaurants, The Chowder Bowl and Swedish Sandwich Shop, were located in this house. (Fran Nichols) Right: The stove of The Chowder Bowl. (Mr. and Mrs. Richard Harris)

Clara's Restaurant

71   South end of Washington Street

c. 1930

Clara's Restaurant was located on the site of Daniel Hall's Tavern at Hall's Corner where the Exxon Station now stands. Clara Redmond and Hazel Mount were in business together in the 1940s and early 1950s. James Queeny recalls them serving "outrageously good food . . . for $1.00." Blueberry pie and lobster salad were specialties.

This restaurant was so small that kitchen vapors would permeate the little dining room. One customer recalls the trouble she had with her glasses steaming up when she came in to have lunch. Clara advised her, "If you would just back through the front door when you enter, you won't have any more trouble." The customer did, and the advice worked!

After the restaurant closed, the building housed a real estate office. Then the structure was moved to the Baptist Church on Tremont Street and used for their Sunday School. For this small building, the prayers seem to have come after eating!

Clara's Restaurant was originally on the site of the Exxon Station at Hall's Corner.   (Fran Nichols)

The Corner Coffee Shop

72 Hall's Corner

1960

The Corner Coffee Shop in the brick building built by Levi Cushing at Hall's Corner was opened in May, 1960 by Eugene Redlon and Elmer Glass. The restaurant opened each day at 6 and closed just before dinner. However, during snow storms, Gene, who was known for his great sense of humor and friendliness, stayed open all night for the men who were operating the plows.

In April, 1971 Marie Heiblinger purchased the shop. A very capable manager, she was not afraid of hard work. People in town stopped in regularly for a cup of coffee. Dorothy Wentworth recalls, "many lasting friendships were made as a regular fraternity developed." Marie's fans and friends were so disappointed to hear that she would be forced to vacate after the building was sold in 1981 that they gave her a farewell party at seven o'clock in the morning!

The building has been completely renovated and filled with many shops.

An aerial view of Hall's Corner taken in 1966. *(Hilton and Hilton)*

Further Acknowledgments

Mr. and Mrs. B. Duncan Adams
Dr. and Mrs. Robert Allio
Doris Beal
Mr. and Mrs. Edwin Brewer
Mr. and Mrs. Thomas F. Burgess
Mr. and Mrs. James W. Callanan, Jr.
Mr. and Mrs. Ralph Carver
Mr. and Mrs. Timothy Coffey
Mr. and Mrs. John M. Dahlen
Mr. and Mrs. Richard Dillon
Mr. and Mrs. William Dixon
Mr. and Mrs. Marsden Earle
Mr. and Mrs. John Ferreira
Marie Fox
Nancy Glass
Mr. and Mrs. Edward S. Grant
Bobby Hackett
Louise Hadley
Mr. and Mrs. John Hagerty
Priscilla Hall

Priscilla Harris
Mr. and Mrs. Richard Harris
Guy Holbrook
Mr. and Mrs. Robert A. Hutchinson
Mr. and Mrs. James R.W. Jenner
John Johnson
Dr. and Mrs. Sylvester Kelley
Mr. and Mrs. Edward Knecht
Mr. and Mrs. Walter Kopke
Mr. and Mrs. Richard I. Lamere
Mr. and Mrs. Frank B. Lawson
Mr. and Mrs. Timothy Leland
Larry F. Lenrow
Madeleine S. Leonard
Robert F. Lonegran
Mr. and Mrs. Hayden Mason
Mr. and Mrs. Alton J. Matinzi, Jr.
Mr. and Mrs. Joseph McGrath, Jr.
Mr. and Mrs. Alexander Molino
Jorgen S. Nielsen

Dr. and Mrs. Vernon D. Patch
Ethel Pearce
Marjorie Phillips
Mr. and Mrs. Andrew Pollock
Augusta C. Randebrock
Mr. and Mrs. William Rice
Jan Schwartz
Mr. and Mrs. Joseph Shea
Mr. and Mrs. John E. Sheehan
Doris Simkins
Mr. and Mrs. E.E. Solomon
Eleanor S. Sprowl
Mr. and Mrs. David Stookey
Mr. and Mrs. Jack Stevenson
Mr. and Mrs. David H. Thompson
Donald R. Thompson
Mr. and Mrs. Elden Wadsworth
Mr. and Mrs. Richard Wadsworth

Footnotes

1. Nathaniel Shurtleff and David Pulsifer, eds., *Records of the Colony of New Plymouth in New England*, 12 vols. (Boston: 1855–1861), XI: 195.
2. Ibid., 137.
3. Ibid., I: 99
4. Ibid., I: 75, 106; II: 43.
5. Ibid., V: 53.
6. Justin Winsor, *History of the Town of Duxbury, Massachusetts, with Genealogical Registers* (Boston: Crosby and Nichols, 1849), 305.
7. Ibid., 305
8. Ibid., 47
9. Ibid.
10. "Richard Lowden," Dateboard Notebooks, v III, #108. Virginia Seaver, Researcher. Duxbury Rural and Historical Society.
11. Virginia Seaver, Researcher.
12. Henry David Thoreau, *Cape Cod* (New York: Bramwell House, 1951), 178.
13. Mary Caroline Crawford, *Old New England Inns* (Boston: L.C. Page, 1907), flyleaf.
14. Pauline Winsor Wilkinson, "Life in Duxbury, 1840," Duxbury *Clipper*, 8 May, 1975, 6.
15. From a hotel brochure.
16. Name is misprint, should be Prior.
17. Willard deLue, "Readers Cast Light on Monitor Roof, Lava Blocks," Boston *Daily Globe*, 15 March, 1954, 13.
18. *Old Colony Memorial*, 3 December, 1898.
19. Pamphlet issued by Mr. C.M. Reade.
20. *Duxbury Town Record*, 2 January, 1883.
21. Ibid., 15 March, 1884.
22. The name *gurnet*, according to Winsor, p.29, comes from gurnet fish found off the coast of Devonshire, England.
23. John Bradford, "A Vanished Industry" (Manuscript, Duxbury Rural and Historical Society, 1893), 10.
24. Ibid.
25. Jerusha F. Hathaway, *Duxbury Sketches* (Dorchester, Mass, Underhill Press, 1921), 24.
26. Bradford, 10.
27. Samuel Eliot Morison, *The Maritime History of Massachusetts* (Boston: Houghton Mifflin, 1924), 103.
28. Laurence Bradford, *Historic Duxbury in Plymouth County, Massachusetts* (Boston: Fish Printing, 1900), 68.
29. Duxbury *Pilgrim*, 20 June, 1890.
30. Advertisement in the *Pilgrim Town of Duxbury* (Plymouth, A.S. Burbank, n.d.)
31. *Pilgrim Town of Duxbury* (no publisher, 1896), 19.
32. *Annual Report of the Town of Duxbury for the Financial Year Ending March 15 1875*, (Plymouth: Avery and Doten, 1875), 52.
33. From a post card advertising Homewood.
34. Agnes Repplier, *To Think of Tea!* (Boston: Houghton Mifflin, 1932), 194.
35. Ibid., 195
36. "Highway and Police Regulations," *Annual Report of the Town Officers and Committees of the Town of Duxbury, 1905* (Plymouth: Memorial Press, 1905), 46.
37. From a post card advertising Mary Hackett's.
38. James Westaway McCue, *Cape Cod Holiday* (Silver Lake, Mass, 1944).
39. Henry Fish, "Tarkiln and Chandlertown, Fordville and West Duxbury" (Manuscript, Fish Notebooks, Duxbury Rural and Historical Society), III: 158
40. Ibid.

Bibliography

Annual Reports of the Town of Duxbury. Duxbury: 1840–1960.

Crawford, Mary Caroline. *Among Old New England Inns.* Boston: L. C. Page, 1907.

Duxbury Rural and Historical Society Collections. Pauline Winsor Wilkinson, "Life in Duxbury–1840." ts (1921). —Plymouth Abstract and Title Co. *Historical Commentary*, n.d.

Duxbury Town Records. Town of Duxbury, 1772–1922.

Earle, Alice Morse. *Stage Coach and Tavern Days.* Williamstown: Massachusetts Corner House, 1977.

Etheridge, George, ed. *Copy of the Old Records of the Town of Duxbury, Massachusetts from 1642–1779.* Plymouth: 1893.

Fish, Henry. *Duxbury Ancient and Modern.* Duxbury, 1924. —"Notebooks." 3 vol, n.d. Duxbury Rural and Historical Society.

Hathaway, Jerusha. *Duxbury Sketches.* Dorchester, Mass: Underhill, 1921.

Long, E. Waldo, ed. *The Story of Duxbury, 1637–1937.* Duxbury: Duxbury Tercentenary Committee, 1937.

McCue, James Westaway. *Cape Cod Holiday.* Silver Lake, Mass: 1944.

New England Historic Genealogical Society. *New England Historical and Genealogical Register.* v.1- Boston: Samuel Drake, 1847

Perry, E.G. *A Trip Around Cape Cod; Our Summer Land and Memories of My Childhood.* Boston: Charles S. Brinner, 1898.

Pilgrim Town of Duxbury. Plymouth: A.S. Burbank, n.d.

Pilgrim Town of Duxbury. Brochure. No Publisher, 1896.

Repplier, Agnes. *To Think of Tea!* Boston: Houghton Mifflin, 1932.

Resident and Business Directory of Duxbury and Kingston Massachusetts. Boston: Union Publishing, 1915.

Shurtleff, Nathaniel, and David Pulsifer, eds. *Records of the Colony of New Plymouth in New England.* 12 vols. Boston: William White, 1855–1861.

Thoreau, Henry David. *Cape Cod.* New York: Branwell House, 1951.

Wentworth, Dorothy. *Settlement and Growth of Duxbury, 1628–1870.*

Duxbury: Duxbury Rural and Historical Society, 1973.

Winsor, Justin. *History of the Town of Duxbury, Massachusetts, with Genealogical Registers.* Boston: Crosby and Nichols, 1849.

AUTHOR'S NOTE: Newspapers consulted included the Duxbury *Clipper*, 1950 to present and the *Old Colony Memorial*, 1850 to present.

Index

Credits not accompanying each illustration are from the collection of the Duxbury Rural and Historical Society.